Technology, Power, and Social Change

Technology, Power, and Social Change

Edited by

Charles A. Thrall
Jerold M. Starr
University of Pennsylvania

Lexington Books
D.C. Heath and Company
Lexington, Massachusetts
Toronto   London

International Standard Book Number: 0-669-81422-9

Library of Congress Catalog Card Number: 72-2017 *Oct. 7, 1975*

Table of Contents

Preface

For the past eight years the University of Pennsylvania has provided financial support to its International Affairs Association for the purpose of holding an annual national conference on an important contemporary issue. Recent conferences have focused on, for example, Political Justice, Student Political Power, and European Integration. The student director of the 1971 conference was Mr. Ronald Aminzade, then a senior at the University and presently a graduate student in Sociology at the University of Michigan. Aminzade, in collaboration with other students on the Association's planning board, decided to make Technology and Social Change the theme of their conference.

As a student of ours, Aminzade naturally solicited our advice on the organization of the various panels and selection of the appropriate speakers. Insofar as the vital intellectual and social problem of the relationship between technology and social change is one which has been of great concern to the editors, we were very pleased to help plan this important event. From the outset, however, Aminzade and his enthusiastic colleagues in the Association did the lion's share of the work in putting this excellent conference together. In fact, we were so impressed with the quality of their efforts, especially the high caliber of the participants they invited, that we only decided to arrange for publication of the conference proceedings well after other work was underway.

One of our primary considerations in deciding to publish was that a much wider audience than could physically attend the conference would benefit from the provocative exchange of views which we thought would and, subsequently, did take place. We received ample confirmation for this sentiment in the large number of professors and students from other universities who either requested permission to tape record the conference with their own equipment or to buy tape copies directly from the conference organizers. Although the universities were the largest community segment represented at the conference, we can safely say that there were people there from many walks of life, from places all over the country.

Once we decided to publish, we then proceeded to outline and describe the book we saw taking shape. Our work consisted of arranging for publication permission from the participants, tape recording the symposia, transcribing and carefully editing the tapes, and composing the appropriate summary chapters. The editing was done to improve the readability of the printed text while, at the same time, preserving the spontaneity of the original event. We wish to make it clear that we shared equally in the preparation of this book and are equally responsible for whatever credit or blame it warrants. Professor Thrall's name is listed first because somebody's had to be and because the study of technology is somewhat more central to his professional interests.

Along the way, many people helped to facilitate this whole enterprise. In addition to Ronald Aminzade, we wish to thank the other student members of the International Affairs Association who worked so vigorously to make the conference the success that it was: Mark Freedland, Gerry Friedman, Laurie Goldman, Betsy Harris, M.J. Maynes, Robert Meyer, Karl Perkins, Ezra Rosenberg, and Muffet Shayon.

We would also like to acknowledge the following University of Pennsylvania faculty who so generously consented to serve as moderators for the four symposia: Philip Pochoda of the Sociology Department *(Technology and the Counterculture)*, Robert Rosen of the History Department *(Technology and Authority)*, Robert Louis Shayon of the Annenberg School of Communications *(Technology and Humanism)*, and Michael Zuckerman of the History Department *(Bureaucracy: Centralization and Decentralization)*.

Finally, credit must go to E.C. van Merkensteijn, Director of the Language Laboratory of the University of Pennsylvania, who arranged for the taping of the conference, Lynne S. Leicht who transcribed the tapes, Doris Sklaroff who typed the manuscript, and Alicia Civitello who did the proofreading.

Charles A. Thrall
Jerold M. Starr

Technology, Power, and Social Change

1

Two Views on Technology and Man

Lewis Mumford

While I recognize it an honor to be asked to give the keynote address of this conference, various burdens and penalties qualify such an honor and diminish a little one's natural gratification. Inevitably, some of the ideas I express will challenge certain conventional views about the relation of technics to human development: views that have too long been taken for granted without sufficient critical reappraisal. So at the outset I must beg the forgiveness of my colleagues when they find me questioning—sometimes brazenly rejecting—what are for them almost sacred texts and honored rituals. By the same token, I must make clear, as novelists do in order to prevent their fictional characters from being mistaken for real persons, that I do not represent—or knowingly misrepresent—the views of the other participants. For good or bad, this is strictly a solo performance.

That personal embarrassment is, however, a minor matter. My real difficulty springs from quite another source. I probably would not have been chosen for this role, but for the fact that one part of my life-work has been to interpret freshly the relation of technics to social change: not just during the last century or so, but throughout the entire course of human development. For at an early stage in my studies I found that I could not understand many contemporary institutions and activities without tracing them back to what often proved very remote, sometimes prehistoric events. Unfortunately most of our thinking today in technocratic circles is being done by one-generation minds bedazzled over our immediate successes with nuclear energy, moon-shots, and computers—however isolated these feats are from the total historic culture that made them possible, and from man's many non-technological needs, projects, and aspirations.

Naturally those who think this way do not thank me for pointing out that their so-called Industrial Revolution did not begin in the eighteenth century: that on the contrary the "new wave" in technology began as far back as the eleventh century; and that the invention of the mechanical clock in the fourteenth century did more to advance modern technics than the steam engine or the automatic loom. For the clock, on its very face, unified our whole conception of time, space, and motion, and laid the foundation in its exact measurements by standard units for the astronomical-mechanical world picture that still dominates our minds and our daily activities.

Despite later reenforcements from historians like Lynn White, Bertrand Gille,

1

and Fernand Braudel, this well-documented revision of the standard technological clichés has not been generally accepted. So it would be presumptuous on my part to look for a more favorable immediate reception for the even more radical revisions I shall make tonight. For I propose to lengthen the historic perspective sufficiently to present a more adequate picture of the relation of technological progress to social change and human development. Instead of celebrating the further expansion and acceleration of technology, on the lines that have ultimately led to the Power System that now governs our lives, I shall endeavor to restore our runaway technology to the ecological and cultural matrix from which it escaped. And so, far from taking the conquest of nature and the elimination of man himself in any recognizable historic form as the inevitable consequence of technological progress, I shall question both the value of the conquest itself and its inevitability. Not least, I shall seek to expose the irrational factors that have led modern man to surrender essential expressions of human creativity that do not conform to the limited quantitative requirements of the power complex.

This task is not rendered easier by the fact that my most recent book on the subject, *The Pentagon of Power*, approaches from many angles and deals at length with the very themes that have been chosen for discussion at this conference. If anything, that is a handicap, for a book that digests the studies of a lifetime can obviously not be regurgitated in a single hour. Yet since what I have to say is grounded on that detailed historic and ideological analysis, it would be stultifying, indeed somewhat dishonest, to make no reference to this work. If it seems lacking in modesty to recall my main divergences from the accepted evaluations of technological progress, would it not be far more immodest on my part to assume that the members of this audience are familiar with my four books on technics, beginning in 1934 with *Technics and Civilization*, and that my learned colleagues, in particular, have already studied *The Pentagon of Power* and have taken time to grapple critically with its leading ideas? What follows is an answer to that rhetorical question.

My point of departure in analyzing technology and social change concerns the nature of man. And to begin with I show reason for rejecting the lingering anthropological notion, first suggested by Benjamin Franklin and Thomas Carlyle, that man can be identified, mainly if not solely, as a tool-using or tool-making animal: Homo faber. Even Henri Bergson, a philosopher whose insights into organic change I respect, so described him. Of course man is a tool-making, utensil-shaping, machine-fabricating, environment-prospecting, technologically ingenious animal—at least that! But man is also—and quite as fundamentally—a dream-haunted, ritual-enacting, symbol-creating, speech-uttering, language-elaborating, self-organizing, institution-conserving, myth-making, love-making, god-seeking being, and his technical achievements would have remained stunted if all these other attributes had not been highly developed. Man himself, not his specialized technological facilities, is the central fact.

Contrary to Mesopotamian legend, the gods did not invent man simply to take over the unwelcome load of disagreeable labor.

All man's technological inventions are embedded in the human organism, from automation to cybernation: automatic systems, so far from being a modern discovery, are perhaps the oldest of nature's devices, for the automatic responses of the hormones, the endocrines, and the reflexes antedated by millions of years that supercomputer we call the forebrain, or neopallium. Yet anything that can be called human culture has demanded, be it noted, certain specific technical traits: specializations, standardization, repetitive practice; and it was early man's positive enjoyment of repetition, a trait still shown by very young children, as every parent knows, that underlay every other cultural invention, above all language. It was this studious technical development of the organism as a whole, not just the employment of man's hands as facile tools or tool-shapers, that accounts for the extraordinary advances of Homo sapiens. In making these first technological innovations man made no attempt to modify his environment, still less to conquer nature: for the only environment over which he could exercise effective command, without extraneous tools, was that which lay nearest him: his own body, operating under the direction of his highly activated brain, busy by night in dreams as well as by day in seeking food or finding shelter.

On this reading, before man could take even the first timid steps toward conquering nature, he first had the job of controlling and more effectually utilizing his own organic capacities. By his studious exploration and reconstruction of his bodily functions he opened up a wide range of possibilities not programed, as with other animals, in his genes. Strangely, it took André Varagnac, a French observer of the archaic folk remains of neolithic culture, to point out that the earliest mode of a specifically human technology was almost certainly the technology of the body. This consisted in the deliberate remodelling of man's organs by enlarging their capacity for symbolic expression and communal intercourse. Most significantly, the only organ that greatly increased in size and weight was the brain. By this close attention to his body even primitive man at a very early moment placed his automatic functions under some measure of cerebral intervention: the first step in conscious self-organization and direction.

Long before man had given pebble tools even the crudest form of a hand-axe, he had achieved an advanced technology of the body. These basic technical achievements started with infant training; and they involved not only repetition, but foresight, feedback, and attentive learning: learning to walk, learning to control the excretory functions, learning to make standardized gestures and sounds, whose recognition and remembrance by other members of the group gave continuity to the whole human tradition. Not least man learned to distinguish in some degree between his private dreams and shared waking realities, and as the forebrain exercised more authority he learned, likewise in the interest of group survival, to curb his blind destructive impulses, to inhibit overpowering rage and fear and random sexuality. Unless man had mastered fear sufficiently to be able to play with fire—a feat no other animal has dared to perform—he would have lacked one of the essential requirements for the survival and spread of his species, since fire enormously increased the number of foods and habitats available for both paleolithic and neolithic man.

The point I am stressing here is that every form of technics has its seat in the human organism; and without man's many artful subjective contributions, the existing physical world operating directly through the medium of earth, air, fire, and water, would have contributed nothing whatever to technology. So it was through the general culture of the human body, not just through tool-making, that not only man's intelligence but other equally valuable capacities developed; and this qualitative culture, with its esthetic expressions, its moral selection and direction, its emotional communion—in short its life-wisdom—was more essential to human development than any special technical advances—from ancient fire-making and tool-making to modern automation, mass production, and cybernation. Almost down to the present century, all technical operations took place within this organic and human matrix: only the most degraded forms of work, like mining, which was reserved for slaves and deliberately treated as punishment, lacked these happy human qualifications. Only today we are beginning to measure the loss we face through our present efforts to remodel the human organism and the human community to conform to the dehumanized standards of the power system.

This leads me to my second departure from technocratic orthodoxy. How is it, I ask, that modern man since the seventeenth century has made technology the focal center of his whole life: why has the Pentagon of Power, motivated by the abstractions of constant technological progress and endless pecuniary gain, taken command of every human activity? At what point did the belief in such technological progress, as a good in itself, replace all other conceptions of a desirable human destiny? To answer this question I have had to trace this power-fed aberration back five thousand years to its point of origin in the Pyramid Age. But first I would call attention to its expression in modern form, in a sign that once greeted the visitor at the entrance of a World's Fair celebrating "A Century of Progress." What that sign said was: Science discovers: Technology executes: Man conforms.

Man conforms indeed! Where did that strange categorical imperative come from? How is it that man, who never in his personal development conformed submissively to the conditions laid down by nature, now feels obliged at the height of his powers to surrender unconditionally to his own technology? I do not question the fact itself. During the last two centuries a power-centered technics has taken command of one activity after another. By now a large part of the population of the planet feels uneasy, indeed deprived and neglected, unless it is securely attached to the megamachine: to an assembly line, a conveyor belt, a motor car, a radio or a television station, a computer, or a space capsule. For the purpose of confirming this attachment and universalizing this dependence, every autonomous activity, once located mainly in the human organism or in the social group has either been bulldozed out of existence or re-shaped by training and indoctrination and corporate organization to conform to the requirements of the machine. Is it not strange that our technocratic masters recognize no significant life processes or human ends except those that further the expansion of their authority and their magical prerogatives?

Thus the condition of man today, I have suggested in *The Pentagon of Power*, resembles the pathetic state of Dr. Bruno Bettelheim's psychiatric patient: a little boy of nine who conceived that he was run by machines. "So controlling was this belief," Dr. Bettelheim reports, that the pathetic child "carried with him an elaborate life-support system made up of radio, tubes, light bulbs, and a breathing machine. At meals he ran imaginary wires from a wall socket to himself, so his food could be digested. His bed was rigged up with batteries, a loud speaker, and other improvised equipment to keep him alive while he slept."

The fantasy of this autistic little boy is the state the modern man is fast approaching in actual life, without as yet realizing how pathological it is to be cut off from his own innate resources for living, and to feel no reassuring tie with the natural world or his own fellows unless he is connected with the Power System, or with some actual machine—constantly receiving information, direction, stimulation, and sedation from a central external source, with only a minimal opportunity for self-motivated and self-directed activity. Man is no longer at home with life, or with the environment of life: which means that he is no longer at home with himself. He has become, to paraphrase A.E. Houseman, "stranger and afraid" in a world *his own technology* has made. But in view of the fact that during the last century our insight into the organic world has been immensely deepened, indeed revolutionized by the biological sciences, why do we still take the Newtonian "machine" instead of the Darwinian "organism" as our model, and pay more respect to the computer than to the immense historic storage of mind and culture that made its invention possible?

Since my own analysis of technology began, not with the physical phenomena of mass and motion, but with organisms, living societies, and human reactions, I do not accept such conformity as anything more than a passing aberration, one of many errors that the human race has committed while straining to improve its condition, and make use of powers and functions it does not even now fully understand. Within the framework of history and ecology one discovers a quite different picture of Nature, and a more hopeful view of man's own dynamic potentialities. Biology teaches us that man is part of an immense cosmic and ecological complex, in which power alone, whether exhibited as energy or productivity or human control, plays necessarily a subordinate and sometimes inimical part as in tornadoes and earthquakes. This organic complex is indescribably rich, varied, many-dimensioned, self-activating; for every organism, by its very nature, is the focal point of autonomous changes and transformations that began in the distant past and will outlive the narrow lifespan of any individual, group, or culture. What is now praised and exalted as "instant culture"—in reality a blackout of memory, similar to what takes place under certain drugs—bears no resemblance whatever to any real human culture, since without some of paleolithic man's basic inventions, above all language, even the latest discoveries of this one-generation culture could not keep in mind long enough to be described, understood, or continued beyond its own ephemeral lifetime.

On this interpretation the all-important problem for technology is not to extend further the province of the machine, not to accelerate the transformation of scientific discoveries into profit-making inventions, not to increase the output of kaleidoscopic technological novelties and dictatorial fashions, not to put all human activities under the surveillance and control of the computer—in short, not to rivet together the still separate parts of the planetary megamachine, so that there will be no possibility of escaping it. No: the important question for all human agencies today, and not least for technology itself, is how to bring back the attributes of life to a system that, without them, will not be able to survive the destructive and irrational forces that its original achievement generated. If our main problem today turns out to be that of controlling technological irrationalism, it should be obvious that no answer can come from technology. The old Roman question: Who shall control the controller? has now come back to us in a new and more difficult form. For what if the controllers, too, have become irrational?

Now how did the Victorian notion—that science and technology, if sufficiently developed, would replace or happily demolish all the earlier agencies of human culture—come about? Why did progressive but humane minds, from the eighteenth century on, think that it was possible and desirable to wipe out every trace of the past, and thus to replace an organic culture, full of active ingredients derived from many varied natural and human sources, by an up-to-date mechanical substitute, devoid of esthetic, ethical, or religious values, or indeed any specific human qualities except those that served the machine? By the middle of the nineteenth century, this belief had become a commonplace. Progress meant, not humanization, as in the earliest technology of the body, but mechanization—with bodily efforts becoming more and more superfluous until they might either be eliminated, or at best be transferred, in a limited way, to sport and play. Was this the inevitable effect of the Industrial Revolution?—and, if so, what made progressive minds embrace so fatalistically the inevitability of the inevitable?

Now, my own generation, accepted readily—all too readily—this faith in the redemptive power of science and technology: though not, I hasten to add, with the fanatical devoutness of a Buckminster Fuller or a Marshall McLuhan today. So, when I wrote *Technics and Civilization* more than thirty years ago, I still properly stressed the more beneficent motives and the more sanguine contributions of modern technics: and though I gave due attention to the ecological depredations of the Paleotechnic phases, I supposed that these life-vitiating practices would be wiped out by the further neotechnic improvements promised by hydroelectric energy, scientific planning, industrial decentralization, and the regional city. Still, even in *Technics and Civilization*, I devoted a long chapter to the negative components which, so far from disappearing, were becoming more demonic, more threatening, and more insistent.

Some twenty years later, in a seminar I conducted at the Massachusetts Institute of Technology, I critically reviewed this early interpretation, and found that the chapter I had devoted to the negative aspects of modern technology would have to be expanded. While all the current praise of industrial rationalization was, up to a point, sound, this had been accompanied by an irrational factor we had not dared to face—or had mistakenly attributed to fascism or communism alone. For during the last half-century, all the concealed symptoms of irrational behavior had suddenly exploded in our faces. This period witnessed not only the outbreak of two global wars, but the further degeneration of war itself into deliberate genocide, directed not against armies but against the entire population of the enemy country. Within a single generation, less than thirty years, thanks to purely technological advances, from the airplane to napalm and nuclear bombs, all the moral safeguards mankind had erected against random extermination had been broken down. If this was technology's boasted conquest of nature, the chief victim of that conquest, it turned out, was man himself.

With these massive miscarriages of civilization in view, I tentatively put to myself a decade ago a question that I did not ask publicly until I wrote the first volume of *The Myth of the Machine*: "Is the association of inordinate power and productivity with equally inordinate hostility, violence, and destructiveness, a purely accidental one?" This question was so uncomfortable to entertain, so contrary to the complacent expectations of our technocratic culture, that I cannot pretend that I eagerly searched about for an answer. But fortunately, at that moment, I was making an intensive study of the whole process of urbanization, that which Gordon Childe called The Urban Revolution, as it took place in Egypt and Mesopotamia toward the end of the Fifth Millenium before the Christian era. Digging mentally around those urban ruins, I discovered an astonishing artifact that had escaped the attention of professional archeologists: an extraordinary complex machine which turned out, on analysis, to be the archetype of all later machines. This artifact had for long remained invisible, because it was composed entirely of highly specialized and mechanized human parts. Only the massive results of its operation remained partly visible, not the formative ideas and mythical projections that had brought this machine into existence.

What Childe has called The Urban Revolution was only an incident in the assemblage of the "megamachine," as I chose to call it. Please note that the superb technological achievements of this gigantic machine owed nothing, at the beginning, to any ordinary mechanical invention: some of its greatest structures, the great pyramids of Egypt, were erected without the aid of a wheeled wagon or a pulley or a derrick. What brought the megamachine into existence was not an ordinary invention but an awesome expansion of the human mind: a transformation comparable to that which took place when in the distant past the structure of language had advanced sufficiently to identify and communicate and pass on to later generations every part of a community's experience.

The decisive tools that made this machine possible were the new inventions of the mind: astronomical observation and mathematical notation, the art of the carved and the written record, the concept of a universal order derived from close observation of the heavens and giving authority—the authority of the gods—to a single commanding figure, the king, he who had once been merely a hunting chief. At this point, the notion of a divinely appointed cosmic order coalesced with the idea of a human order which shared in its godlike attributes. Then both the machine and the Myth of the Machine were born. And therewith large populations hitherto isolated and scattered could be organized and put to work, on a scale never before conceivable, with a technical adroitness and a machine-like precision and perfection never before possible. Small wonder that those divine powers were worshipped and their absolute rules obeyed!

In unearthing this invisible megamachine I was not so much trespassing on the diggings of established archaeologists as flying over them. So far I was safe! But my next move, in equating the ancient megamachine with the technological complex of our own time, caused me to push into heavily defended territory, where few competent colleagues have as yet been willing to venture. This is not the place to summarize all the evidence I have marshalled in *The City in History* and in *The Pentagon of Power*. Enough to point out that the original institutional components of the Pentagon of Power are all still with us, operating more efficiently than ever before: the army, the bureaucracy, the engineering corps, the scientific elite—once called priests and soothsayers—and, not least, the ultimate Decision Maker, the Divine King, today called the Dictator, the Chief of Staff, or the President.

Once I had discovered the megamachine I had for the first time a clue to many of the irrational factors that have undermined every civilization and that now threaten, on a scale inconceivable before, to destroy the ecological balance of the whole planet. For from the beginning, it was plain, the Invisible Machine had taken two contrasting forms, that of the labor machine and that of the war machine: the first magnificently constructive and life-saving, the other destructive, savagely life-negating. Both machines were products of the same original myth, which gave to a purely human organization and an all-too-human ruler an authority—a divine authority, derived from the cosmos itself. To revolt against that system, or try to withdraw from it, was disobedience to the gods. Under very thin disguises, those gods are still with us.

Since the original labor machine was of no use except for large-scale operations, smaller, more serviceable and manageable machines of wood and brass and iron were in time invented as useful auxiliaries to the Invisible Machine. But the archetype itself persisted in its negative, military form; the army, and the army's table of organization was transmitted through history, more or less intact, from one large territorial organization to another—the army with its hierarchic chain of command, with its one-way mode of communication, solely from top to bottom, with its system of remote control, with its regimentation of responses, ensuring absolute obedience to the word of command, with its readiness to impose punishment and inflict death to ensure conformity to the Sovereign Power. Not only does this power system break down human resistance, and destroy the communal institutions that stand in its way, but it seeks to extend both its political rule and its territorial boundaries; for power, whether technological, political, or pecuniary recognizes no necessary organic limits.

The real gains in law, order, and economic productivity the megamachine made possible need not be belittled. But unfortunately these gains were reduced, often entirely cancelled out, by the brutalizing institutions that the military megamachine brought into existence: organized war, slavery, class expropriation and exploitation, and extensive collective extermination. In terms of human development, these evil institutions have no rational foundation. This, I take it, is the basic trauma of civilization itself; and the evidence for it rests on much sounder foundations than Freud's quaint concept of a mythical act of patricide. What is worse, the hallucinations of absolute power, instead of being liquidated in our time through the advance of objective scientific knowledge and democratic participation, have become more universal. In raising the ceiling of civilization's constructive achievements, the megamachine likewise lowered its depths.

The parallels between the ancient and the modern megamachine extend even to their fantasies: in fact, it is their fantasies that must first be liquidated by rational exposure if the megamachine is to be replaced by a superior and more human type of organization and association. In the religious legends of the early Bronze Age, one discovers, if one reads attentively, the same irrational residue one finds in our present power system: its obsession with speed and quantitative achievements and technological exhibitionism, its bureaucratic rigidity in organization, its relentless coercions, its hostility to autonomous processes not under control by a centralized authority. And no wonder! All the boasted inventions of our modern technology first erupted in audacious Bronze Age dreams as attributes of the gods or their earthly representatives: remote control, human flight, supersonic locomotion, instantaneous communication, automatic servomechanisms, germ warfare, and the instantaneous extermination of large cities by fire and brimstone, if not nuclear fission. If you are not familiar with the religious literature of Egypt and Babylonia, you will find sufficient data in the Old Testament of the Bible to testify to the original paranoia of power, in the dreams and daily acts of the gods and the kings who represented that absolute power on earth.

Just as today, unrestrained technological exhibitionism served as proof of the absolute power of the monarch and his military-bureaucratic-scientific elite. None of our present technological achievements would have surprised any earlier totalitarian rulers. Kublai Khan, who called himself Emperor of the World, boasted to Marco Polo of the automatic conveyor that brought food to his table, and of the ability of his magicians to control the weather. What our scientifically-oriented technics has done is to make even more fabulous dreams of absolute control not only credible but probable; and in that very act it has magnified their irrationality—that is, their divorce from the ecological and historic conditions under which life of every kind, and above all conscious human life, has actually flourished. The fact that most of these ancient fantasies have turned into workaday realities—that is, hardware—does not make their present and prospective misuse less irrational.

Do not be deceived by the bright scientific label on the package. Ideologically the modern power complex, if measured by the standards of ecology, is as obsolete as its ancient predecessor. Our present technocratic economy, for all its separate inventions, lacks the necessary dimensions of life economy and this is one of the reasons that the evidences of its breakdown are now becoming frighteningly visible. We have abundant biological evidence to demonstrate that life could not have survived or developed on this planet if command of physical energy alone had been the criterion of biological success. In all organic processes quality is as important as quantity, and too much is as fatal to life as too little. No species can exist without the constant aid and sustenance of thousands of other living organisms, each conforming to its own life-pattern, going through its appointed cycle of birth, growth, decay, and death. If a feeble, unarmed, vulnerable creature like man has become, though at his peril, lord of creation, it is because he was able deliberately to mobilize all his personal capacities, including his gifts of sympathy, group loyalty, love, and parental devotion, gifts which ensured the time and attention necessary to develop his mind and pass on his specifically human qualities to his offspring.

For remember: man is not born human. What has separated man's career from that of all other species is that he needs a whole lifetime to explore and utilize—and in rare moments to transcend—his human potentialities. When man fails to develop the arts and disciplines that bring out these human capacities, he sinks, as Giambattista Vico long ago pointed out, to a far lower level than any other animal. Since the megamachine from the beginning attached as much value to its negative components—to success in war, destruction, and extermination—as to its life-promoting functions, it widened the empire of irrationality. To face this built-in irrationality of both ancient and modern megamachines is the first step toward controlling the insensate dynamism of modern technics.

Let me cite a classic example of our present demoralizing conformities.

Observe what a distinguished mathematician, the late John von Neumann, said about our current addiction to scientific and technological innovations. "Technological possibilities," von Neumann said, "are irresistible to man. If he can go to the moon, he will. If he can control the climate, he will." Though von Neumann expressed some alarm over this situation, I am even more alarmed at what he took for granted. For the notion that technological possibilities are irresistible is far from obvious. As an historic fact, this compulsion, except in the form imposed by the divinely appointed megamachine itself, is limited to modern Western man. One of the chief weaknesses of traditional village communities was rather that they too stubbornly resisted even the most modest technical improvements, preferring stability and continuity to rapid change, random novelties, and possible disruption. As late as the seventeenth century an inventor in Rostock was publicly executed for designing an automatic loom.

What von Neumann was talking about was not man in general, but modern Western Man, Bureaucratic Man, Technocratic Man, Organization Man, Post-historic or Anti-historic Man: in short, our compulsive, power-obsessed contemporaries. Let us not overlook the fact that when any single impulse becomes irresistible, without regard to past experience, present needs, or future consequences, we are facing an ominously pathological derangement. If von Neumann's dictum were true, the human race is already doomed, for the governments of both the United States and Russia have been insane enough to produce nuclear weapons in quantities sufficient to exterminate mankind five times over. Is it not obvious that from the outset there has been a screw loose in the mighty megamachine? And have these paranoid obsessions not increased in direct proportion to the power the system now has placed in the hands of its leaders?

How is it then, you may ask, that earlier civilizations were not destroyed by the persistent aberrations of the military megamachine? The most obvious answer is that their destruction repeatedly did take place, in most of the twenty-odd civilizations that Arnold Toynbee's *Study of History* examined. But insofar as these power systems survived, it was probably because they were still held back by various organic limitations: mainly because their energy, in the form of man-power, was derived solely from food crops; and though sadistic emperors might massacre the populations of whole cities, this killing could be done only by hand. Even in its palmiest days, the megamachine depended upon the self-maintenance of man's small, scattered, loosely organized farming villages and feudal estates, whose members were still human enough to carry on even when the ruling dynasties were destroyed and their great cities were reduced to rubble.

Furthermore, between the power technics of the megamachine and the organic, fertility technics of farm and garden, there mediated a third kind of technics, common to both the urban and the rural environments: namely, the cumulative polytechnics of the handicrafts—pottery-making, spinning, weaving, stone-carving, building—each a repository of well-tested knowledge and practical experience. Whenever the centrally controlled megamachine broke down or was defeated in war, its scattered members could reform themselves, falling back on smaller units, each transmitting the essential traditions of work and esthetic mastery and moral responsibility. Not all the technical eggs were in one basket. Until now, this wide dispersal of working power, political intelligence, and craft experience happily mitigated the evil effects of a system based on the abstractions of power alone.

But note: our modern power system has annihilated all these safeguards, and thereby, incidentally, endangered its own existence. Thanks to its overwhelming successes in both material and intellectual productivity, the organic factors that made for ecological, technological, and human balance have been progressively reduced and will soon be wiped out. Even as late as 1940, as the French geographer Max Sorre pointed out, four-fifths of the population of the planet still lived in rural areas closer in their economy and way of life to a neolithic village than to a modern megalopolis. That factor of safety is fast vanishing, and except in backward or underdeveloped countries may soon disappear. No competent engineer would design a bridge with as small a factor of safety as that under which the present power system operates; and the more completely automatic that system becomes and the more extensive its electronic mode of control, the narrower that margin becomes; for as the system itself becomes more completely integrated, the human components become correspondingly disintegrated, unable to take over the functions they have too eagerly sur-rendered to the machine.

Judged by any rational criteria, the modern megamachine has poor chances of survival. Though everyone is now aware of its mounting series of slowdowns and breakdowns, its brownouts and blackouts, these failures are ironically the results of the power system's very success in achieving unqualified quantification. Technologically speaking, the old problem of scarcity of food or goods has been solved, but the new problem of quantitative abundance has proved even more disconcerting, and harder to remedy without radically revising all the principles of our pecuniary-pleasure economy. The old megamachine worked, we now perceive, only because its benefits were reserved for a small privileged class, or a small urban population. The modern megamachine, in order to justify mass production, has been forced to impose mass consumption upon the entire population. Without deliberate human intervention, vigilantly imposing thrift, moderation, restraint upon the whole business of quantification, the affluent society will choke to death on its waste products. Unless we come down to earth and recover our ecological and human heritage, it will be vain to seek for "pie in the sky by and bye."

Fortunately in recent years there has been a sudden, if belated, awakening to the dire consequences of blind devotion to technologies' expansions and extensions. Who can now remain blind to our polluted oceans and rivers; our smog choked air; our mountainous rubbish heaps; our sprawling automobile cemeteries; our sterilized and blasted landscapes, where the strip miner, the bulldozer, the pesticides, and the herbicides have all left their mark; the widening deserts of concrete, in motor roads and carparks, whose substitution of ceaseless locomotion for urban decentralization daily wastes countless man-years of life in needless transportation; not least our congested, dehumanized cities where health is vitiated and depleted by the sterile daily routine. With the spread of biological knowledge that has gone on during the last generation, the meaning of all these ecological assaults has at last sunk in and begun to cause a general reversal of attitude toward the entire technological process, most markedly among the young. The claims of megatechnics are no longer unchallengeable: its demands no longer seem irresistible. Only backward Victorian minds now believe "you can't stop progress"—or that one must accept the latest devices of technology solely because they promise greater financial gains or greater national prestige.

Happily we do not have to wait for a general revolution to begin dismantling the megamachine and replacing the Power Complex by a balanced biotechnic economy. This has already begun. The decision by our American Congress to waste no further funds on the development of the SST, the supersonic transport plane, is a notable victory for human reason and human values. The fact is that this extravagantly priced toy was conceived solely to inflate the image of a minuscule minority—the technocratic jet set, whose egos were inflamed by the singular illusion that the few hours they might thus save any day in planetary travel would be of value or significance to any other human soul. This may turn out to be an epoch-making decision: for it shows there is no need to turn technological permissions into social compulsions.

By now it is becoming clear that our problem is not to adapt our social institutions at whatever sacrifice of continuity and coherence, to a constantly expanding technology, or to curtail human needs and desires to meet the strict requirements of our mechanized, electronically controlled environment, much as an astronaut is trained to accept the severely restricted existence imposed by a space capsule. Just the opposite: we must bring back into every part of our daily life the autonomous modes of functioning appropriate for living organisms, with all the counter-proposals, the insurgent demands, the orderly disciplines that aim to enhance man's own personal creativity.

Our model can no longer be the machine or the mechanical organization or the electronic system, but the organism, or rather societies and associations of organisms, whose members exhibit the bi-polar activities of all living organisms: change, yes, but change without destroying continuity; growth, yes, but always limited growth; balance, but a dynamic balance, constantly shifting, like the acid-alkali balance in the body; autonomy and self-direction, surely, but autonomy within a general pattern of cooperation and mutual aid; and certainly a plenitude of power, but not unlimited power, only power sufficient to foster the good life. An economy that was conceived on this organic model would be able to utilize to the full all the resources science and technics place invitingly before us, without being overwhelmed by them, or becoming subservient to the Power Complex.

Ironically, in presenting the case for a more balanced conception of technology which would do justice to all the dimensions of human life, I myself have been guilty of unbalance: for I have overemphasized my heresies, my departures from accepted views, and have not done justice to the many minds that have for more than a century been laying the ideological and scientific foundations for just these organic conceptions. I would have reason to feel embarrassed were I alone in bringing forth the ideals of a dynamic, self-balancing, life-oriented economy, for in fact this reorientation began long ago in the thought of Peter Kropotkin, the geographer, of Ebenezer Howard, the modern founder of the New Towns movement, and of my own master, Patrick Geddes, whose views came directly from Darwin and Huxley, both master ecologists. Howard even dared to call his new towns Garden Cities, in the belief that the deliberate marriage of town and country he proposed would lay the basis for a new civilization.

This ferment is now more actively at work than ever before, and in many different areas. Already there are over two dozen New Towns built on Howard's principle in Britain alone, to prove that the landscape need no longer be obliterated and defiled by mass urbanization. Similarly a fresh line of thought can be traced in economics, mapped out by economists like Tawney, Galbraith, and Mishan: a line that actually goes back to John Stuart Mill. Instead of accepting the explosion of population and the expansion of technological inventions as an irreversible condition, the new economy seeks to curb this seemingly automatic process. It aims deliberately at a stable population, on which basis attention and effort would be directed to non-consumable goods, without a price tag or a power tax—the goods of art and education and play—rather than to financial profits and material extravagances. The idea of a balanced economy was put forward by Mill in his chapter on "The Stationary State"; a chapter until now remembered mainly because it was there he observed that it was doubtful if all our labor-saving machinery had actually lifted the burden of the day's work from a single human being. Unfortunately Mill broached the idea of a dynamic balance in an offhand way, and under a misleading title, probably because he realized it would be dismissed by his Victorian contemporaries as a heretical effort to disparage the benefits of technological progress.

Though Mill did not carry his idea further, it has recently been bobbing up again in various places: I myself called attention to it in 1938,[1] and again in 1944,[2] when it seemed that in the West a slowdown in population growth was actually taking place. Today, the Center for the Study of Science and Society at Albany, New York, under the direction of Dr. Eugene Rabinowitch, has instituted a series of studies on the possibility of what he, as a physicist, has called a Steady State Society—a term unfortunately almost as lacking in organic connotations as Mill's Stationary State. But the change of mind indicated by these efforts is significant, for they break with the original premises of the megamachine, both ancient and modern; namely, that its power system is irresistible and that the most irrational fantasies of the Power Elite must be respected and obeyed: above all, the religious belief that the incessant inflation of power and profit and productivity are more important than all the other functions and purposes of life.

But where shall we go to find an organic model which will eventually displace the underdimensioned mechanical model which took possession of our minds and dictated our behavior for the last three centuries? If I have probed this situation deeply enough I have already implanted the answers in your minds, though even with the help of my *Pentagon of Power* you may take some time to recognize all its implications, and a still longer period to work out an effective response that can be transformed into action. As my final word—and it must be only a final word, not another lecture—I would refer you back to my earlier discussion of the nature of man, and of the part that repetitive mechanical discipline itself played in bringing out all man's varied bodily capacities, in modes of creativity that transcended his animal limitations. We must restore to the human organism many of the work-functions we have transferred to the machine, for much of our boasted labor-saving has proved life-defeating. The problems that have been raised by our dehumanized technology cannot be solved by the system that created them. They are essentially psychological, religious, and moral problems, though no historic religion or philosophy ever fully succeeded in starting them, still less in mastering them. It is perhaps only now, with the aid of the historic perspective and evolutionary insights we have acquired during the last century, that an effective effort can be made in creating a unified, organic world picture; a picture that does justice to both the patent and the latent potentialities of organisms, communities, and human personalities.

Happily, in recognizing the primacy of moral and religious renewal as the essential condition for any future technology that will contribute to man's culture and humanization, I am again not alone. While preparing this paper, I was encouraged to find that Georges Friedmann, in his new book *La Puissance et La Sagesse (Power and Wisdom),*[3] had come to essentially the same position I have reached, almost in the same words: a remarkable development in an outstanding sociologist of modern technics, indeed a world authority. Even more remarkably, Friedmann had begun his intellectual career as a Marxian determinist, skeptical of any higher order of reality incarnated in the human personality itself. And almost at the moment of writing these final sentences, Irving Kristol, an American scholar, not a professed moralist but a sociologist, writing in the magazine section of the *New York Times*, in a masterly analysis of the moral debasement and internal disruption of our society, has re-affirmed the central function of morality as the only defense against our continued brutalization and dehumanization: the Pornography of Power, from Auschwitz to My Lai.

In the very nature of things, a discussion like this must be teasingly spotty, superficial and unsatisfactory; and even the series of substantial books that stand behind what might otherwise seem only loose generalizations, are themselves almost equally teasing, to me no less than to my most attentive and enchanted readers. But if I have done my job properly, I have set you thinking on another course than that which was summed up in that slavish tribute to the Myth of the Machine I quoted earlier: "Science Discovers: Technology Executes: Man Conforms." *Does* man conform? *Must* he conform? *Will* he conform? *Should* he conform? The last question involves man's nature, his historic development, his self-transformations, his conscious pursuit of values and purposes that transcend both his animal self and the technological pressures and automatisms of his immediate environment. Once one asks that last question—*should* he conform?— the problems raised by technology are restored to a truly human perspective. But *will* man conform? That question has yet to be settled; and—speaking to each of you as a representative of mankind—my final word is: the answer lies in your own hands.

Notes

1. Lewis Mumford, *The Culture of Cities* (New York: Harcourt, Brace, 1938).

2. Lewis Mumford, *The Condition of Man* (New York: Harcourt, Brace, 1944).

3. Georges Friedmann, *La Puissance et La Sagesse* (Paris: Gallimard, 1970).

Robert Theobald

I was trying to get one of my telephone calls through one evening and as so often happens these days I got cut in on another line. Two people were talking to each other. One said, "We have just run the latest data through the computer and it proves that there is a one percent chance of survival for the human race." I listened a little bit longer and discovered that I was listening to two Martians who were discussing what possibilities there were that the world might start making intelligent decisions.

They then talked Martian for fifteen minutes and when they started talking English again they said: "Isn't it a pity that the human race doesn't know that."

What I am going to try to do is to explain in English some of the things that the Martians said. It's going to take me more time than it should because English is an extremely bad language. Robert Heinlein has pointed out in several of his books that English is an illogical language, based on a set of premises and assumptions which are incorrect. It is therefore extremely difficult to talk sense in English or, indeed, any Western language.

I believe that in my role of a Keynote Speaker I should engage in the process of opening questions rather than closing them. It seems to me that our greatest problem today is that we assume that we know things that we do not know. We act as though questions are closed when they should be open. Indeed we do not perceive most of the relevant questions because we think in obsolete categories.

The university is ideally designed to insure that you remain certain that you know the answers to obsolete questions. The university and the schools are designed to teach you answers to questions that other people posed long ago. The problem today is that the questions we should be answering are not yet known. Unfortunately the process required for discovering the right questions is totally different from the process for discovering the right answers.

Take my own discipline of economics. It is assumed in neo-classical economics that all firms are small, there are no labor unions, there is perfect movement of information, and there is no government intervention in the economy. I would suggest that this is a less than adequate description of the American society today! However, if these assumptions are false, we are no longer entitled to argue that everybody gets the amount of income to which he is entitled. One of the keystones of our economic policy today falls of its own weight. Economics is, in fact, a branch of politics. The amount of money you get is roughly determined by your amount of power.

The second set of assumptions that we have is neo-Keynesian. This states that there is no change in the quantity or quality of technology, no change in the quantity or quality of the labor force, and no change in equipment. Surely, this is also a less than adequate description of the situation today! And yet this is the theory on which our assumptions about the possibility of permanent full employment are based.

It should surely be obvious that we need a new set of assumptions relevant to today's reality. And until we discover a relevant set of assumptions, what we are learning is actively dangerous: not merely neutral, but actively dangerous. (I am talking here about the social sciences.)

But does learning or knowledge make any real difference? One of the last audiences I spoke to was at Madison, Wisconsin. I suggested that knowledge could change the way the world operated. This statement created a buzz saw of negative comment. Paul Sweezy, a Marxist, had said earlier that we needed a revolution and we couldn't have one. I said we needed fundamental change, that we had better find a way to achieve it, and the only way I knew to get real change was to alter people's conception of their self-interest.

This may not seem to be a very dramatic statement at first sight. Its significance becomes clearer if it is translated into the statement of John Maynard Keynes who said "In the long run it is ideas and not men who rule the world." What we think is in our self-interest depends on what we perceive.

Let me cite two rather significant recent changes in perceived self-interest in this culture. And then let me try and sort out some of the implications of these changes, some of the issues that they raise. The first of them is the supersonic transport. The supersonic transport is a much more significant issue than people have yet been willing to face up to. Those in favor of a better environment are arguing on the basis of this one decision—that Congress *can* deal effectively with the complex issues of the communications era. This is surely over-optimistic. The reasons the supersonic transport went down to defeat have very little to do with the benefits and dangers of the supersonic transport itself.

There has been a change in mind set from assuming that everything that science and technology can do is good to almost assuming that everything that science and technology can do is bad. I would suggest to you that one oversimplification is as dangerous as the other. Maybe it would be nice to go back to a time when each of us had our own green field and our own untouched spring and our own little house somewhere off in the wilderness. For better or worse, however, there are already three and a half billion of us on this planet and there are going to be a lot more before we stop the population explosion. We are not going to feed, clothe, and shelter that number of people without science and technology.

The Neo-Luddite Revolt, (Luddites being the British who smashed machines in the nineteenth century) goes very deep. It goes deep because of the romantic belief that we can somehow go back to an untouched environment. It goes deep because of a fear of unemployment by people just like you, who are aware that the jobs are not there and that machines are going to take their jobs away from them.

Those of you who read science fiction know that one of the most fundamental issues in science fiction has been the computer revolution, the robot revolution. (I find it very interesting that it was usually robots in science fiction. Maybe this is because science fiction writers are intellectuals and they don't want to think about computers which take over brain work, but only about robots which take over manual work.) It is the computer revolution which is hurting. And a great many of you are being trained for instant obsolescence. So naturally many try to keep the machines away: Keep them away, above all, from teaching.

Teaching is probably the field where we could use computers most. Not, of course, for education, but for training. Why don't we use them? Because too many teachers are aware that they are merely computer surrogates and that what they presently teach could be just as efficiently programed onto computers. There's the classic joke about the professor who tape-recorded his lectures. He arranged to put his tape recorder down on the university podium. At the end of the semester he came back and found that his tape recorder was facing a whole row of student tape recorders. Far too many teachers are simply output devices. This function can be far better served by computers and films and programed learning.

The killing of the passenger SST, therefore, stems from a fundamental change in mind set. It symbolizes a change from a world in which Americans believed that anything which science and technology could do was good. Ten or twelve years ago everybody thought the space program was a great idea. We believed that anything that could be done should be done. And so we went to the moon. A lot of rationalizations have since developed in terms of spinoffs and benefits. But the real reason we went to the moon was that man felt that if the moon was there, we should get there. Today, we think differently.

The second change, and this one hit probably much closer to the heart of America and the world, is the conviction of Lt. William Calley. Because this fundamentally and basically undermined structural authority, which is basic to the operation of the present industrial-era society. Our society is based on the right of a man at the top to give orders and the certainty the orders will be obeyed. We placed a delayed time bomb under that system at Nuremberg when we said that there is a distinction between legal and illegal orders. (You can take this evaluation back one step if you wish to that case at the end of the Civil War where a man was killed for obeying legal orders.) But at Nuremberg we made it clear that there is a distinction between a legal and an illegal order.

Such a view is great in theory—until you're fighting a war. Who then decides what an illegal order is and what a legal order is? Supposing, for example, you had been in Vietnam at the time of the Cambodian invasion, and you had studied international law and believed that it was illegal to invade a neutral country. Should you then refuse to participate in the invasion? Or, more immediately, supposing you were ordered to kill "civilians," should you refuse?

Those who have been in the military may perceive that the position is impossible. The reaction to the Calley conviction stems from this situation. It is why, among other reasons telegrams are running 150 to 1 against his conviction.

Let us assume Calley *should* have been convicted. In this case, where do you stop? Do you convict the other veterans who are turning themselves in across the country—because they say that they did similar things? Do you convict the U.S. commanding general? A Japanese general was held responsible for atrocities in his command of which he did not know. Should everybody who participated in the My Lai massacre be tried? But then what about other massacres that took place in Vietnam?

It may seem that I am laboring the point, but I don't think I am. Vietnam has dramatized the effective disintegration of the organizing principle of the industrial era. It is not only the military that runs on structural authority. If there is such a thing as an illegal order in the military, why can't the principle be extended to argue that the order received from the president is illegal?

Such a process has, in reality, been developing throughout the society in recent years. Structural authority, the right to command because of position has been disintegrating. Some surprising people have been speeding this process. One of the key people in the process has been Vice-President Agnew: he has been destroying the structural authority of the media. Previously it was accepted by many that a commentator on a network, or an editor on a newspaper, had the right to tell people what to believe. Fourteen years ago, it was sufficient to read the *New York Times* to know "what was going on."

Today, young people argue that position does not of itself give a right to make decisions for the society. Black people, women, homosexuals, the old, the young are making the same basic statement. "We will not be ruled by people whose only right to make a decision is the post they hold."

Such a statement seems unbearably threatening to many. We have got so caught up in the industrial era that we cannot imagine any other form of authority than structural. We assume that if we abolish bureaucratic authority, the whole world will necessarily fall apart.

The total lack of anthropological sophistication in the United States leads Americans to argue with sublime certainty that one cannot change human nature—they mean that there is only one way to behave—the way Americans behave. Even young people say this, despite the fact that they are participating in one of the most fundamental shifts in "human nature" that has ever taken place. Human nature is extremely maleable.

The SST and the Calley case demonstrate the end of the industrial era—despite this reality the society is still trying to put it together again. Those of us, on the other hand who are trying to create a new era consonant with the new realities are considered outside the acceptable intellectual framework: more often we are bluntly referred to as "nuts." The intellectual magazines in this society, like *Harpers*, the *Atlantic*, the *New York Review of Books*, are still in the industrial era. There is no presently existing way of moving information about the new world effectively. Those of us who are trying to think about the new world cannot find each other and therefore cannot work together because we don't yet know how to communicate.

Let me now try to separate three ways of looking at the future.

The first way, the only way that was visible until recently, is the extrapolist school. When I first started writing in the late fifties, people were still assuming ever-continued growth. People were quite seriously predicting that in the year 2000 there would be 30 million cars produced each year. Nobody seemed to worry very much where the 30 million cars would go or, indeed, as far as I could see, whether there would be enough people to drive all of them at the same time. (In the months since this paper was presented, I have discovered that we have learned even less than I thought about the fact that never-ending extrapolist curves are impossible of achievement.) For example, Herman Kahn in his latest book on Japan[1], seems still to be saying exactly the same thing. He argues that there has been a 10 to 12 percent growth rate in Japan for many years and that it is going to continue. The Japanese, in the months since the book has appeared, are attacking it because they have decided that there are such things as consumer problems and environmental problems which may make a high rate of growth less than attractive.

Nevertheless the extrapolist concept remains the accepted academic view of the future: the future will be like the past only more so. It will be bigger and brighter and brassier. Philosophy students will recognize a classic statement of determinism, raised from the private to the social level. There is nothing that can change the future; it has been determined by the past; you had better learn to live with it. This is the thesis of Alvin Toffler's book *Future Shock.*[2] (I think it is possible to see why the book is so popular. It permits people to dream themselves back into a vanished era: to feel that the industrial era will continue. *Up the Organization*[3] carries the same message. It permits managers to argue that they should go back and *really* apply the Protestant Ethic.)

We can understand what is happening better if we recognize the anthropological thesis that there is a flourescent, developmental, classical, and degenerative stage for each culture. However the industrial culture lasted for a shorter time than any other. It is, therefore, not surprising that a lot of people are still seeing the industrial era as in its classical period, when actually it has gone already passing through the degenerative stage. We must produce a new culture if we are to survive.

We must change rapidly. There's no effective way to prove this statement, but some indicators can be given. Consider how the recent small California earthquake cut a rather substantial hunk of that state off from the United States for a significant amount of time. And yet our war planning is still based on the assumption that a hundred million people can be killed, the major centers of population of the United States can be destroyed, and the United States will still survive as a functioning entity. It is conceivable this view was valid when war planning was originally done for the nuclear age: it is not true today. The socio-techno-economic system is too complicated and it gets more complicated every day. For example, it seems certain that one or more of the germ laboratories would be broken into during a nuclear holocaust. We shall either learn to create "peace," which is not merely an absence of war—or we will not survive.

There is another possible disastrous scenario. The world will come to perceive itself as split between the rich and the poor, the white and the non-white—both internally and externally. We're very close to this situation at the present time. This could only lead to disastrous violence.

The second view of the future which is very popular today, is put forward by Charles Reich in *The Greening of America.*[4] If all of us should become Consciousness III People, the world will operate beautifully. (Consciousness III can be defined as "good people," "religious people," "groovy people," depending on your language.) The trouble with Reich's statement is that it has always been true. If everybody became religious or good tomorrow, we would solve our problems pretty quickly. I would suggest to you, however, that the odds on this happening are no better now than they have been in the past.

The Reichian view leads to some very fascinating consequences. I spent three days with a theologian recently. We thought we agreed with each other when we started our discussions but we found how much we disagreed with each other by the time we were through. This theologian believes that man, society, reality are totally flexible. For example he believes and I quote, "Man has no sex drive." He argues that man is "taught" about sex: that without a culture he would have no sexual concerns.

He became very disturbed when I said that man is fundamentally a great ape. For him man is a spiritual being. I would argue that our only hope of becoming a spiritual being, is to accept where we start from, to accept the reality of our genetic inheritance. I believe it is fatal to our chances of human growth to assume we are something we presently are not. Similarly, if we hope to change our society from being what it presently is to being the sort of society I believe we can create, we had better look at our present situation as honestly as possible.

If we really do want fundamental change, we will only bring it about by evolutionary means. Past revolutions have changed titles and positions but they haven't changed anything fundamental. I would suggest to you that Russia after the revolution is very similar to Russia before the revolution: that France after the revolution is very similar to France before the revolution. If we want to achieve revolutionary change, it must be achieved in an evolutionary way. I was taught this lesson by Conrad Arensberg, an anthropologist who showed me that revolutionary change could only occur by evolutionary ways. The Chinese did not invent gunpowder to kill people: they used gunpowder to open Temple doors. The people who domesticated cattle presumably didn't think they were domesticating cattle. I am sure they simply thought this was a convenient way to hold a cow or bull until they were ready to eat it.

If you, therefore, want to manage social change, you have to manage it in such a way that change appears evolutionary but has revolutionary potential. We must therefore act in an ahistorical or non-historical way if we are to survive. History shows that other cultures confronted with massive change in the past have failed to change. So long as we try to act "historically" we have no hope. If we tackle our present situation in historical terms, we shall certainly fail—in this case, this meeting and all similar meetings are irrelevant. If we are to be successful—i.e., ahistorically—we have to do something which has never been done. We must change fundamentally people's sense of their own self-interest. In other words, we have to change people's sense of reality.

What does this mean? We have always made a mess of discussions about reality because we have argued about whether reality "exists" or does not. There is no immediate answer to this question. However, we can find a question which can be answered.

Let me ask you to look around this room and imagine that you are a giraffe, or a fly, or a cat, or a dog, Chinese if you are white or black, white or black if you are Chinese; male if you are female, female if you are male. What would happen in each of these cases to your perception of this room? Each of us picks out certain relevant things about this room and we call that reality. The number of facts in this room—even the fairly obvious ones, let alone the esoteric ones—is far more than we can take in and still continue to operate successfully. Let me make the same point in a different way. When driving down a road, your vision of reality is totally different when you're a passenger and when you're a driver. We always chose "the reality" within which we operate. It is our choice of reality which determines what we perceive and the future we create.

It is in this sense that Teilhard de Chardin, the Catholic theologian, and a growing number of geneticists and biologists are correct in saying that you "pull" yourself into the future by your choice of the things perceived and not perceived. This is why the statement that professors can determine for students what they will benefit from learning, misses the point. Each one of us must discover our own route into the future by choosing those things which meet our present needs.

Let me make a parenthesis here. Most university students, when they arrive at the university, are incapable of learning to learn because their high school experience has not taught them the necessary skills. Neither of the present styles we use as students enter the university deal with this reality. For example, Antioch and other similar colleges act as though people are really full grown adults and can do everything: this is profoundly destructive if the necessary skills for reality perception do not yet exist. Other universities in general act as though students are not adults and not capable of obtaining adulthood. This is equally immoral. If we really want to change the university, we are going to have to develop a freshman first year which will give people the skills required to learn to learn. In my opinion we must teach the ability to think in various modes, a crash course in social reality, and a course in what I call arting, the ability to create something with your own hands and to value it for what it is. When students have the skills taught in these classes they can start to learn. At that point, people have got to make decisions about what they want to learn. Because nobody else can make them effectively although everybody can get help from other people.

To survive, we must change our conception of reality. We have to create a new view of man. I believe, in particular, we must face up to new definitions of life and death. Many present policy questions, for example the abortion question, are obviously insoluble in terms of the present set of images we are using. The question of senility, and people lying in nursing homes waiting for death, is also insoluble.

Death used to be automatic: we have now created a situation where death often has to be permitted. Mankind is going to have to learn when to be born and when to die. And this in a culture which has tried to abolish the visibility of death.

I am not able to provide answers as to what the new definitions of life and death are. I will, however, suggest the way that my own thinking goes. Life exists when you can contribute to your own growth and to the growth of other people. Death is when you cannot do so and when your life subtracts from your own development and that of other people. I believe we shall come to feel that when one cannot contribute, and is destroying other people's lives, then death is something that one will not only accept but welcome. In other words, life is a communication process. It is a process by which you discover other people, you help them to grow; you grow yourself. Life has nothing to do with chronological age. Some of the people I know who have been most alive, have been old in chronological terms.

I fear I'm going to be misunderstood. To prevent this result to the maximum extent I should make it clear I am not talking about compulsory euthanasia. I am not talking about "big brother" deciding when you are ready to die.

This new attitude toward death is symbolic of a much broader shift. We are going to have to make our own decisions in the most difficult areas: we are going to have to give up the belief that others can solve our problems. The credential, hierarchical society is dying.

To put it bluntly, in different terms, it is quite clear that a Ph.D. is becoming counterproductive in many ways, even measured by whether one can get a job or not, because Ph.D.'s are now often seen as overqualified—a perilous thing in our society.

The university began to break down when people decided that they would not be put on a "conveyer belt" and come out rolled in their B.A. The system began to collapse when people decided that they were human and awkward and had corners, and demanded to be treated as individuals. The system cannot be put back together again.

Let me, therefore, imagine a new communications-oriented university for one moment. The catalog is a fascinating relic. Why do we have catalogs? Because the only way you could circulate information was to put it on a printing press. Putting it on a printing press took a very long time. So you had to get everything straight and simple. There were two semesters of four months each. Every piece of knowledge, every piece of learning had to take four months. What alternative is there? We could go to a corporation, which has surplus computers, obsolete for their purposes, but suitable for ours. We then use the computer to set up a system in which people who want to take the same course take that course, the course runs just as long as people want to take the course—when it ceases to be useful it ceases to be listed on the computer. On the other hand, when a group of people want to take a new course, it is listed on the computer. The computer uses visual print-out devices to keep people informed.

Let us look at another area. We are still taking nine months to print books. A computer system, coupled to a rapid output printer, could produce books very rapidly and produce them as ordered instead of having additional copies sitting in warehouses. And so books can be kept up to date. However, nothing will happen without a conceptual breakthrough in any of these areas.

It may be easiest for me to summarize the beliefs of my wife and myself about the future by summarizing the timetable in *Teg's 1994,*[5] in which we have tried to describe some of the issues of the next twenty-five years. This book summarizes where we think we might go if we try hard, but not hard enough. In other words, this is not a utopia, but a survival scenario. (Teg is a young girl of twenty who is awarded an Orwell Fellowship in 1994. The Orwell Fellowships were created in 1984, because the world wasn't in such quite bad shape as it might have been.)

The seventies in this scenario were a time of fundamental breakdown of the society. The breakdown was caused first by the Neo-Luddite Revolt, which I've talked about; second, by a consumers' revolt, a decision that you can't add value to goods by advertising; third, by very rapidly growing tension between the developing and the developed countries—between the countries in the abundant regions and the scarcity regions. America is seen as becoming increasingly isolationist. (I worked with the United Nations last year at the time of the announcement of the Second Development Decade. There was no major coverage anywhere in America.) Fourth, *Teg's 1994* assumes that the educational system will fall apart during the seventies: that many colleges, schools, universities will close. They will close partly because people will no longer find them relevant and the brighter students will leave; this pattern is already developing. In addition, we have already moved into an acute financial crises. (Teg suggests two ways out of this crisis. One is for the university to move back into the community, for more and more classes to be taught in the community; for more and more teachers to come out of the community; for more and more students to come out of the community. The second possibility is for the university to concentrate on a specific problem/possibility: much as the University of Wisconsin is concentrating on ecology.)

At the end of the seventies, two key breaks occur in the scenario. One of them is what we call the Scientists' Synergy. When the Scientists' Synergy occurs people refuse to put out inaccurate or distorted information to please their employer or anybody else. The Scientists' Synergy occurs in 1979: it creates a massive change in the whole culture. It is difficult to overestimate the impact of such a change, for lying is now basic to our culture. Just look at the terms we use: management of the news; public relations, that's the word that colleges, churches, any other groups use for their own peculiar form of distortion; and advertising.

This acceptance of lying is moving us into the Tower of Babel II: a situation where nobody believes anybody else. There is a classic story about two psychiatrists who went up in the elevator together. As they left, the elevator man said to them, "Good morning." As they walked down the hall one of them said to the other, "Now, what did he mean by that?" I think that story symbolizes where we are at the communication process. We can't hear anything. We're looking for motives under motives under motives. Any of you who have ever been to a psychiatric faculty meeting will know what happens in that situation.

The other break in the scenario happens in the early eighties when goods and services become free. Some of you have argued for a guaranteed income. However, a guaranteed income—and income maintenance which I consider equally important at this point for middle level managers, engineers, etc.—is not the long-run answer. The long-run answer is to recognize that money no longer works as an effective allocation mechanism. Why? The answer is simple. We pay people for the disutility of their work. In theory, I get paid because I don't like doing what I'm doing. But *I* do like doing what I'm doing. And there's no reason why computers and technology will not permit us to reach the point at which everybody does what he wants to do: and doesn't do more of it than he wants to. There is another side to the coin. If we can produce enough to go around, why should people pay for it. Some of you know the old science fiction story, *The Midas Plague* by Frederick Pohl, that in x number of years, we will reach a point where the poor will be forced to consume and the rich will be allowed not to. The time is not so far away. Do you doubt that we can provide a decent standard of living to everybody in this culture with our present technology? I don't have any doubts.

This is why my dream is that we can feed, clothe, shelter, and permit all people to find their own dignity long before the end of this century. There is no good reason why this shouldn't happen except that we lack the will to act. We can solve all our problems if we learn to operate on the basis of a communication model and not on a power model.

It is naive to believe that I—or you—can significantly influence any issue on which power is already being exercised. In other words, if we are already in a situation where an issue is of concern to a great many powerful people and organizations in this culture, it's going to get settled on a power basis. Communication is therefore irrelevant. However, we can influence other issues which lie in the future by communicating about them if people with power are not yet interested.

We have a choice to make. Within the conventional model, those who do not use power cannot expect to achieve change. Within the model I use, we must recognize that others have—and will have—more power than us and that we can only create change by changing the views of those with power about their own self-interest. My experience shows that this task is far less impossible then is generally assumed—many of the most powerful are also most aware of the growing breakdown of our culture and the need to change their definition of their self-interest.[6]

Notes

1. Herman Kahn, *The Emerging Japanese Superstate: Challenge and Response* (Englewood Cliffs: Prentice-Hall, 1970).

2. Alvin Toffler, *Future Shock* (New York: Random House, 1970).

3. Robert Townsend, *Up the Organization* (New York: Knopf, 1970).

4. Charles Reich, *The Greening of America* (New York: Random House, 1970).

5. Robert Theobald and J.M. Scott, *Teg's 1994* (Chicago: Swallow Press, 1971).

6. The views expressed in this paper are so different from the conventional norm that all their implications cannot be explored here. Following many requests, a special package of books by Robert Theobald is available from Personalized Secretarial Service, 5309 North 7th Street, Phoenix, Arizona 85014, for the special price of $7.50. Checks must accompany order.

2 Symposium on Bureaucracy, Centralization, and Decentralization

Victor C. Ferkiss

What I have to say may seem startling and far out simply because it is so commonplace. But it is sometimes useful to know where we are and how we got here before we try to ascertain where we are going.

I may be wrong, but I think that for most people in America today—certainly for most people at this conference—bureaucracy is a dirty word. This is likely to be true regardless of whether one is pessimistic or optimistic about technology. For many persons pessimism about technology includes the fear that it will make this terrible thing called bureaucracy stronger or more pervasive, while optimism entails the belief that technology will somehow make possible liberation from the thralldom of bureaucracy. If this is true, then before we talk about the relationship between technology and bureaucracy we must first gain a realistic understanding of the nature of bureaucracy and its impact upon society.

It is hard for many people today to recognize that bureaucracy came into the world—the Western world at least—as a liberating force, as did its concomitant, administrative centralization. Everyone now is so into the idea of community, face to face contact, and total relationships that it is hard to accept the fact that much of the Western past has been devoted to the attempt to break away from these very things.

The King's peace came to localities in England and Europe as an alternative to the often arbitrary rule of the lord of the manor, an alternative eagerly welcomed by the common man. Centralization, written law, and fixed rules were originally regarded as liberating. This is equally true with regard to the segmented kind of personal utilitarian relationships which so many people deplore. Just a few years ago, though it now seems much longer than that, theologian Harvey Cox wrote a popular and influential book called *The Secular City*,[1] celebrating among other things the impersonality of relationships in the large modern technopolitan metropolis. Since then he has changed his mind at least once, but many persons would still argue that there is much to be said for centralized bureaucratic power. If you are a black in Mississippi you are a lot better off dealing with a federal court operating under formal and universalized rules than with a local sheriff operating on the basis of personalized local criteria. But most of us today—and this is not purely a matter of intellectual fashion—fear impersonal power, segmented relationships, and all the other alleged evils we associate with bureaucracy.

29

Bureaucracy and centralization have historically gone hand in hand, both made possible by technology. Technology provided the kinds of communications devices which made the governing of large empires not only possible but easy. It made possible all the apparatus of reporting, inspection, conferences, and coordination which are part of any modern bureaucratic state. Technology allowed for the meticulous record keeping required by taxation, conscription, and public health and education. When Max Weber describes the essence of modern bureaucracy—in a tone overlain with a pessimism which has had much to do with influencing the attitudes of subsequent generations of intellectuals toward bureaucracy—he is describing a system for which modern technology is the necessary if not the sufficient condition.

With technologically-conditioned modern bureaucracy came centralized and hierarchically organized power. The dominant rule of capital cities over political life and of major industrial and commercial centers over economic life was greatly strengthened. And, as Weber noted, hierarchical relationships—power at the top and obedience at the bottom—were a basic feature of the bureaucratic systems themselves and of the political and economic systems of which they were the instrument and underpinning.

But does the fact that in the past technology has been the source of hierarchical, centralized, bureaucratic political and economic systems mean that this must always be the case? Might not new forms of technology change these relationships and make possible a greater degree of decentralization, local autonomy, and individual freedom? New forms of physical power—especially electric motors—have made possible a high degree of decentralization of productive processes as compared with the early days of the industrial revolution. It can be argued that most of the economic centralization in industry today is the result of financial rather than technological considerations, that it is not physical but market conditions that give the giant corporation its competitive advantages. In the same vein, new technologies have led to a greater decentralization of population within existing metropolitan areas. Some would argue that Mr. Mumford's dream of garden cities is, ironically, already with us in the nightmare of suburbia, made possible by the automobile's decentralizing impact upon patterns of population settlement.

Beyond this, modern technology has made possible dispersion of control centers as well as of population. Some urbanologists would argue that this is an oversimplification, that birds of a feather continue to flock together, that even if Gulf Oil can have its technical headquarters in Houston and service your credit card from there, its executives want to have their real headquarters on the same blocks in New York where the big banks are. Many industrial and especially financial and intellectual activities still remain concentrated. But it is now technologically possible to run a large modern state from anywhere, from a San Clemente or Florida "White House" as well as from Washington. And certainly it is not necessary to have every activity run from the same location, even if individual activities are run from central headquarters. The National Institutes of Health are not in Washington, but in suburban Maryland; the Pentagon is in suburban Virginia; the Space Flight Center in Houston; the Strategic Air Command in Colorado; and so on. Communications today make it possible for individuals to operate from almost anywhere and for societies to be controlled from almost anywhere. There is a tremendous amount of choice possible.

But wherever it is located, centralized direction has its problems; problems which, paradoxically, are created by the very improved technological means which make a high degree of communication possible. The more information coming into a central place, the more decisions which can be referred to a central headquarters, the greater the information and decision overload. This is not a wholly new problem of course. It used to be said that the Emperor Franz Joseph of Austria-Hungary used to try to read and sign every important government document himself and as a result was five years behind when he died. However apocryphal, this story illustrates how bad things could get just using ordinary pen and paper supplemented by the telegraph wire. Paradoxically, the vast technological advances of the mere half century since Franz Joseph's time have so confounded the problem of administration that it is harder to get needed information than ever before.

Some years ago I spent some time working for the Peace Corps, an agency which was essentially dependent on the State Department's worldwide communications system. Sooner or later, no matter how sophisticated the electronic equipment used, the messages all ended up in the State Department's communications center. At that point they would be picked up by some low-paid clerk, possibly with fallen arches, who would then wheel them around the building in the equivalent of a supermarket shopping cart. The result of course was that it took much longer for messages to get from downstairs to upstairs to their intended recipients than from India to Washington. We used to resort to such unbureaucratic practices as virtual bribery of the people in the mailroom to get our messages faster and to cut down on the possible two days required to receive a message requesting action within hours. No matter what sort of sophisticated techniques might be devised to bypass the mail sorters and the people with the carts, sooner or later any message is going to be another piece of paper—or tape or whatever—on someone's desk, and the more efficient we are in getting paper there the more difficult it becomes for the receiver to cope with it.

Nor is information overload the only block to centralized direction of large scale activities created by improvements in communications technology. The larger an organization, the more efficient its internal communications, the more things to coordinate as far as decisions are concerned and the harder it is to get agreement and consistency. There is so much business to be transacted that in order to avoid information and work overload officials must rigidly and arbitrarily narrow their fields of attention, as a result of which decisions are made by subcenters of power which are mal-integrated or even directly at cross-purposes with each other. This kind of counterproductive activity will also occur in large organizations as a result of political power considerations, independently of technological factors, as when the Agriculture Department helps export tobacco and cancer to our friends abroad at the same time the Surgeon General's office is trying to curtail tobacco-caused cancer at home. But communications overload makes the situation much worse.

Suppose one wanted to overcome the difficulties caused by information overload in order to make more efficient social control possible? Does technology offer any options for solving some of the problems it has helped to create or acerbate? Recent concern with the interrelated problems of our cities and the ecological situation of our planet as a whole has led to a burst of interest in the possible use of the computer as a tool for mapping, or modeling, or managing large systems. A computer is essential to handle the vast number of variables involved in systems analyses of the kind proposed by such theorists as Jay Forrester, which involve operations too complex for the unaided human mind.

Would the perfection of such computer technology, enabling us to better understand what is going on in the complex systems of which we are a part, lead to structures which are more centralized, more bureaucratic, and more hierarchical than those which so many deplore at present? Not necessarily. Organic unity and efficient communication—which may be necessary to planetary survival—may not require as much hierarchy and centralization as sometimes assumed.

Our oldest organic theories of government go back to Plato, who compared the body politic to a human body, its organs under the control of man's mental faculties. But while it is true that a good deal of the time our voluntary muscles are controlled by deliberate intellectual decisions—and it may be possible that many more aspects of our physiology are subject to mental control than we have heretofore believed—Plato's analogy between the human body and society is based on a false premise. From the biologist's point of view, the body is a complicated system of information feedback where much of what is thought in the brain depends on the signals it gets from nerves, glands, and other sources. The body is far more democratic than Plato realized.

Thus, if by bureaucracy one means a necessarily hierarchically controlled organization, it is possible to conceive of a system possessing a high degree of coordination which is not really bureaucratic in the usual sense of the word. Information technology could be devised which could make everyone a participant in social decision making even at the national or world level. People could participate in coordinated large scale communal activity without the feeling that they were mere cogs in an engine operated from outside, or simply pawns being pushed about by unreachable, unmovable leaders.

If freedom means absolute individual or local autonomy, independent of the desires and needs of the larger community, then freedom cannot exist in the modern world. But if freedom is conceived of as effective participation in coordinated decision making, involving a high degree of understanding of what is actually going on, it may be possible. Kenneth Boulding talks about the need to move from a cowboy economy to a spaceship economy if our densely populated, highly interdependent world is to survive. But it is equally important that we move from a cowboy mentality about politics to a spaceship mentality, which recognizes that understanding and participation rather than isolation and complete independence is the essence of freedom.

In summation, then, bureaucracy as it has existed in the past is going to change radically—or at least can be radically changed—as a result of new technological options. New possibilities exist which can help us cope with the major political task of our age: the creation of mechanisms adequate for dealing with the problems of an interdependent world while at the same time permitting the individual a measure of freedom, power, and control of his own identity and destiny. Technology, however, can never do more than provide us with possibilities; the task of choosing is our own.

Notes

1. Harvey Cox, *The Secular City* (New York: The Macmillan Company, 1966).

Murray Bookchin

It is my intention here today to challenge the fundamental assumptions that have justified hierarchy, bureaucracy, elitism, and a centralized technology, both in the past and in our own social period. For, I submit, unless we break away from these assumptions—unless we challenge these assumptions completely and unrelentingly—we will fail to make any significant steps toward a humanistic use of technology or a humanistic society.

Allow me to cite an example of what I mean. If Victor Ferkiss says that bureaucracy played a relatively liberating role during the feudal period, I would be obliged to add that bureaucracy—liberating or not—has always been a form of hierarchy. Perhaps it was liberating (as the "king's justice") in an historical period when nobles exercised arbitrary power, but it still played this role within the framework of domination. Bureaucracy was—and still is—based on the assumption that there are those who are to be vested with the authority to make decisions in society and others who are obliged to obey these decisions. Bureaucracy was—and still is—based on the assumption that there are those who are equipped to manage and govern society and others (the great majority, in fact) who take orders. Perhaps in an historical period—when technology was so undeveloped that material surpluses were so marginal that only enough existed to provide free time, security, and self-cultivation for a small minority, making class domination an inherent feature of social life—bureaucracy and centralization were unavoidable. We have gone far beyond those harsh material conditions today, yet we continue to use the concepts and categories of that distant, technologically undeveloped social period. We still assume that decisions have to be made by the few for the many; that the individual stands in contradiction to the collective; that the claims of individuality stand opposed to the conditions of communism.

I want to challenge all of these assumptions. I want, in fact, to work with an entirely different set of assumptions. Doubtless, there may have been a time when bureaucracy played a somewhat "liberating" role. But today bureaucracy is not only unnecessary and not only is it possible to do away with it, but it is absolutely *necessary* to do away with it. And the same holds true for centralization. Allow me to emphasize, here, that my concern is not with efficiency. My concern, first and foremost, is with a society that will create the atmosphere for completely liberated human beings who, in their "individualism," will not regard their relationships with other human beings in terms of competition and conflict. We tend to look upon differences in hierarchical terms; whatever is "different," "unique," or variegated is viewed as "better" or "worse" than something else. Living in a time when differences between people imply conflict, when sexual differences imply domination, and when economic differences actually result in domination, we tend to hold the spurious belief that any kind of uniqueness, separateness, or variety must result in hierarchy.

Accordingly the differences between the sexes are utilized to justify the domination of women by men; ethnic differences are utilized to justify the domination of blacks by whites; age differences, the domination of the young by older people, and so on. Ecology has taught me to totally reject this tendency to make hierarchies out of differences. I have learned from ecology, in fact, that diversity is a precondition for stability and that the more diversified the system, the more complex the system, the more fully developed is its unity. My experiences as an anarchist, in turn, have taught me that the tendency to cast differences in terms of hierarchy are simply calculated attempts to foster the domination of women by men, blacks by whites, the young by the old, and one social class by another.

What is unique about our own time is that it is not only possible to do away with hierarchy—and, I would add, with bureaucracy, centralization, and property—but it is absolutely *necessary* to do so. And it is necessary to do so if only to deal with the ecological crisis that hierarchy, bureaucracy, centralization, and property have produced. The prevailing hierarchical, bureaucratic, centralized, and propertied society—marked as it is by industrial gigantism and motivated as it is by production for the sake of production—is not only dehumanizing society and depersonalizing the individual, but it is ruthlessly pitting humanity against the natural world. This society is now producing a monumental crisis in the relationship between humanity and nature. The bureaucratic organization of industry, which is reflected by the bureaucratization of political and social life, has become totally anti-ecological. The earth is now being ruthlessly exploited by this bureaucratic system. Not only is this system polluting the earth, but it is literally devastating the entire planet. Like an impersonal machine of destruction, it is blindly devouring raw materials and wasting resources on an incredible scale. This bureaucratic capitalistic system even dominates the very people who think they rule society. They themselves are shaped by it; they themselves are its creatures; they themselves are its products—as shoddy and as spurious as the very commodities the economy produces. If we do not find some way of existing in harmony with the natural world, we will destroy the bases for our own existence on this planet.

But to achieve harmony with the natural world presupposes that we achieve harmony in the social world. Our attitude that man must dominate nature emerges above all from the domination of man by man. The attitude we project upon nature stems from the social relations that exist between humans. The notion that we have to conquer nature stems from a hierarchical society that is based on domination—be this between sexes, age groups, ethnic groups or the inherent forms of economic exploitation that follow from a class and propertied society. Nor can we any longer confine our discussions merely to the need to "diminish" bureaucracy and centralization. We must *eliminate* bureaucracy and centralization, and above all, hierarchy and domination. We must do this not only institutionally and structurally, but in our very attitude toward each other and toward the natural world. We have to talk about the sweeping revolutionary changes in society and in ourselves that will finally eliminate domination in *all* its forms.

The conditions for making these sweeping changes exist today. Ironically, they exist precisely because of the enormous productivity—indeed, the excessive productivity—we have achieved as a result of technological development. Today, these immense technological facilities have a centralized and bureaucratic framework. We must now take them in hand and tailor them along non-hierarchical, decentralized, ecological lines. Nor is the present technology the only kind that is available to us. Side by side with the centralized technology a new one—a smaller, shall we say "miniaturized" one—has emerged which I discussed many years ago in my essay "Toward a Liberatory Technology."[1] As I pointed out in that essay, industrial gigantism is obsolete even from the standpoint of the present industrial system. The traditional centralized technology, like the old coal-steel technology, has been exhausted historically and must be replaced by new sources of energy, decentralized industrial facilities, and entirely new values in the production of goods.

The same, let me emphasize, is true of our cities. Our cities are no longer viable urban entities. It is preposterous to talk about cities today in terms of the great urban traditions that played a liberatory role in the past—urban communities that brought people together and made it possible to create a fund of knowledge that could advance human culture. Cities today are in fact areas of anonymity and isolation, not communication and contact. They are urban belts, not communities. In no sense do they have the cohesiveness and form that cities had in the late Middle Ages or in classical times, during the period of the Athenian polis. Today, we are faced with the total disappearance of the urban tradition and all that it stood for. Centralization has reached a point where the very logistics of urban life are breaking down, not to speak of the massive pollution produced by the great metropolitan areas in all parts of the world. The city as we have known it historically has reached its limits and must be transcended.

Finally, and perhaps most importantly, a critical tension is developing today between what exists and what could be. This tension is most visible in the counterculture created by young people—one which is increasingly influencing adults. The irrationality of the present social system is becoming one of the most compelling factors in creating broad movements for personal and social liberation. The social and the personal, here, are virtually indistinguishable from each other. The attempt to seek personal freedom from the irrationality and inhumanity of the existing system has profound social implications. By the same token, there can be no social liberation any longer without personal liberation. Here, too, technological development has played an indirect and somewhat negative role. We feel we are living in an insensate world of commodities and false needs; in fact we feel deluged by objects to a point where we ourselves are reduced to objects. In increasing numbers, people of all age groups—old as well as young—feel a desperate need to break away from the reification of human life and experience, from the conversion of people and values into merchandisible commodities. Many thousands of people are leaving traditional ways of life and the cities to experiment with new forms of decentralized communal existence. For them the cities have already broken down and are nothing more than pest-holes for individual and social degradation. They are trying to break away from the hierarchical attitudes, values, and modes of life that have not only divided the sexes, races, and age groups against each other, but that have also divided mind from body, town from country, individual from community, society from nature, and even the individual from himself. They are seeking new forms of community that will once again restore the unity of experience and human relationships in a more organic and rounded way of life.

To sum up: I have argued that we have to reexamine all the underlying assumptions that enter into what I would call the hierarchical outlook toward society and the natural world, toward the very concept of difference or diversity. Perhaps hierarchy had some sort of social function when there was not enough materially to go around, when the only type of social system that could exist had to be based on privilege. But today we produce so much that privilege has to be enforced. The entire state machinery must be mobilized to force people to work and the domain of toil must be perpetuated at a time when it is becoming increasingly obsolete. I have also argued that hierarchy is not only obsolete but literally threatens the stability of the planet; that a society based on privilege, domination, production for the sake of production, and, I might add, consumption for the sake of consumption, threatens the integrity of the entire natural world. A new society must come into existence that will respect each individual as a sovereign participant in a free decentralized community, scaled to human dimensions. It will be necessary to decentralize cities into new types of ecological communities based on new ecological technologies—ecocommunities and ecotechnologies as I've described them in my writings—each community living in balance with the ecosystem in which it is located.

Is this "utopia"? Yes—emphatically so. But we can't afford anything less than utopia any longer. The conflict between survival and life has become so poignant, so deep, and so far-reaching in our time that if we don't begin to live, we will literally not be able to survive.

Notes

1. Murray Bookchin, "Toward a Liberatory Technology," *Post-Scarcity Anarchism* (Berkeley, Calif.: Ramparts Press, 1971).

Max Lerner

Beyond technology and beyond power, beyond centralization and decentralization, I think we would all agree that there are just two elementary questions. One is about society. I would certainly agree with Mr. Bookchin when he speaks of the difference between what is and what can be. I call myself neither an optimist nor a pessimist, but a possibilist. I think in terms of what can be, but I think you also have to give your sense of the inner nature of things. Thus, the first question is what is the nature of society, and what is the kind of society we can get? Second, what is the nature of the human being, man himself? And what can be done on the much more intractable problem of reshaping the human potential?

These two questions have haunted me as I've listened to both of my colleagues. I'm sure these are questions they have had to face in their own thinking.

Our problem in long range terms is to go from what we have called *Homo faber* to *Homo ludens*, from man the technician and fabricator to man playing. Listening to the statements we have just heard it occurred to me that part of *Homo ludens* is man's vision. For we have witnessed a moving and imaginative vision, and are moving toward it. I identify strongly with those elements of the new cultural thrust (whether you call it counterculture or Consciousness III, or whatever else) which can give us some of what has just been depicted for us. However, I'd like to give my own view both of the nature of society (and with it technology, centralization, power, and all the rest) and the nature of man.

Let us start with one element which is central to the conference—technology. As technology changes it has two sets of consequences. First, changes in technology set other social changes in motion. You don't have to be a determinist, whether Marxist or Veblenian, to agree that the current far-reaching social changes have largely been set in motion by technology. Second, technology brings with it a certain mind set. I want to discuss both, both the mind set and the larger setting of social change.

I have a thesis here. It comes partly out of a massive book of mine on American civilization.[1] I'm trying to rethink it now in terms of what has happened in the last ten or twelve years, and follow it by a brief sequel. But I am convinced that what I tried to say in the earlier book is being borne out now—namely, that America is probably the most revolutionary society in the world today.

This may sound somewhat startling to those who regard America as deeply reactionary. But I have had the experience, as I have traveled around the world a bit, of having people speak to me about "this reactionary America of yours." I answer; "If you mean you don't like our leaders and their decisions that's your privilege. Many of us don't like them either. But if you mean that America is itself a reactionary society, I say no. It is probably the most revolutionary society in the world today."

Of course the meaning I give to "revolutionary" is not the classical-historical meaning of overturning a regime, of subverting a power structure by organized violence, of achieving a transfer of power from one elite group to another. I mean something different. Mr. Theobald said that revolutions don't change much except labels, and that the problem is to change things in such a way that the changes will appear evolutionary but will in fact be revolutionary. I find myself in agreement with that, just as I agree with a recent book published in Paris, which will soon be translated here, by Jean-François Revel. He calls it *Without Marx or Jesus; the American Revolution has Begun.*[2]

The "Jesus" in Revel's title refers to the European tradition of a Christian revolution. This is also behind Jacques Ellul's thinking on technology, which is basically theological thinking. Defining technology as the sum total of all of the rational means by which you try to achieve a desired effect, he sees it as a kind of devil inside the human being. Immoral technology, immoral man. Like many others whose thinking is not as openly religious as his, he wants to extirpate this particular devil from the human being. I don't happen to think this is a devil to be extirpated. There is an essential and healthy core of man which is *Homo faber.* If there were not we could scarcely have survived those successive historical crises of human survival that Lewis Mumford spoke about in his *Transformations of Man.*[3] My feeling is that he could not have survived if there had not been the element of *Homo faber* in him.

We have now reached the point where the technological element is being pushed so hard that it carries a destructive danger to man himself. But while I believe this, it does not mean that the technological can be extirpated. It is as much part of man as *Homo ludens* is—the thrust toward the playful, imaginative, innovative. It is as much a part of man as the cognitive, which Emerson spoke of when he said the American scholar is "man, thinking." Beyond the cognitive, there is the interrelationship between action and thought, which Bergson meant when he spoke of thinking as men of action and acting as men of thought. That too is part of man. Finally, there is the deeply irrational thrust in man. Aggression and destructiveness are not just the creation of capitalism, technology, imperialism, centralization, and the rest: they are deeply part of the human animal, the whole genetic strain in human history. We must reckon as clearly with that as with technology and centralization. It is in these terms that I look at America today. What is happening in America is not just a revolution in the sense of a coup d'état. As Mr. Theobald said, such revolutions don't change much except captions, as witness the Soviet revolution. But in a much deeper sense, when you get a transformation of institutions ripe for change (as they are in this country), and of social structures and attitudes, then we are in the midst of a deeply revolutionary society.

That is the setting. And the technological set in that setting, I think, is easier to change and there is more of a possibility of changing it than if that setting were not as fluid as it is. In other words, what I'm saying is that the America that we have been witnessing in the last decade is not a "stationary state" (in John Stuart Mill's phrase), or a state trying to walk into the future backward. It has never been as open to change as it is today. Such an American situation gives us a better setting to achieve changes in our technological sets. We have a better chance than ever to move the emphasis from *Homo faber* to *Homo ludens* and to man thinking.

One thing to discard is the notion that we have fallen away from Eden, that there is somehow a serpent in the garden which has corrupted us. There was no Eden. After spending some time wrestling with American history I must report that there never was an Eden in America. From the very start you find struggle, conflicts, inequalities, injustices, domination. Even the story of what happened to the environment has been, from early times, a walk on the wild side. In studying Thomas Jefferson I have become convinced that no small part of the rape of the continent can be traced to the consequences of his ideas and the mind set he represented. This great humanist, this hero of the radicals, this man who felt deeply related to Nature, who hated the cities, who was one of the originators of the anti-urban anti-intellectualism which has run like a thread through American intellectual history—this man cannot escape responsibility for what later happened to the environment. If you take Jefferson's basic thinking, and that of the generations he influenced, you will find a belief in a state of nature ("Nature and Nature's God," as he said in the *Declaration*) and in the laws of harmony between Nature and society. It is on these laws of harmony that the theory of civil liberties and civil rights is based, in a broad doctrine of natural rights and natural law. But also, it followed from these laws of natural and social harmony that governments—federal, state, local—had to keep their hands off the economy. This is the laissez-faire idea as it came down in American history, and while Adam Smith gave it an economic formulation in England, the shaping influence on it in America was the Jeffersonian philosophy of natural law and harmony. As a result, in the single minded pursuit of profit and power, we burned down the forests, depleted the resources, eroded the soil, piled up profits, built the big corporations—all in the name of humanism and of Nature and Nature's laws.

What I'm saying is that we are caught, not just in capitalism, but in the radical tradition itself. What is true of all of us is a kind of ambiguity both in history and in the present. This is a case where we cannot get rid of either technology or power—and any notion of a society getting along without either strikes me as woolgathering.

While we must play down the power structure, *and* decentralize power, and decentralize the administration of technology we're not going to get along without them. Yet it is an irony of history that we are caught in the consequences of them not because of evil institutions or evil men or evil ideas, but because of the evolution of the whole of our social and intellectual history, not only in terms of capitalism and power, but also in terms of radicalism and a kind of grass roots democracy.

That is the nature of the human situation. The beginning of wisdom in these things is to get away from absolutism and to understand the polarities in the human situation and indeed in man himself and in society.

I take one more step. It has been said repeatedly that we must see man's relation to nature in terms of how he has tried to dominate nature and society. We need to correct course, rethink our relation to nature, and see man as a part of the total harmony of nature. Man is part of the total complex scheme of nature, so much so that he needs less hubris, less sense of our right to expect whatever we wish from Nature. We need to see the organic relationship of the whole web of nature, including man. Whatever we do in pursuit of the technologies of the future should be pursued in that spirit of humility rather than of hubris.

But we need to see society as an organism in the same way. There is a new relevance, in the history of thought, for those thinkers—Coleridge, Burke, Tocqueville are examples—who tended to see society as an organism. Like all complex organisms, society is terribly fragile, easy to disturb and destroy, but once destroyed terribly hard to put together again as an organism. If you take a basically engineering approach to society, ripping this out of its context, inserting that, you lose a sense of humility about society and man's relation to it. I plead as much for the need to abandon hubris in our attitudes toward society as for the need to abandon hubris in our attitudes toward nature.

Such is my basic approach. The danger is absolutisms of every kind. We need to free ourselves of absolutisms because one of their consequences is the doctrine of "anything goes." If you are certain that you have a pipeline to the final truth, and are sure of your goals, then anything goes on your means.

On the question of magnitudes, I should like to see them broken down. It is good, for example, to find around the nation an effort to build smaller college units within the multiversity. I regard myself as an anarchist in one sense: I should like to see us circumvent the state, the big corporations, the big trade unions, the big universities. I should like to see us find compassable face-to-face units and relationships and let these institutions develop their technology within that frame.

But the danger about technology lies not just in its magnitudes and impersonality, but in our eagerness to internalize its values. W.H. Auden once said there are two kinds of people, those who live and those who are lived. Many of us have allowed ourselves to be lived—by the giant corporations, the giant state, the giant computer—to be lived by their values, to internalize those values.

To the extent that the new counterculture rejects this internalizing of technological values it is healthy. If we can internalize different values—those of the radical humanist tradition—we can live *with* our technologies, instead of living *by* them.

It may be in order to add something about the Calley case. It has to do with the thrust of the irrational, which I talked about earlier. It is interesting to note the appeal that has been taken from a smaller military jury to the larger consensual jury of public opinion today in the country on the Calley verdict. It is striking to see a large segment of American opinion somehow making almost a hero of this blurred, confused, banal young man. The banality of evil, which Hannah Arendt discussed in the Eichmann case, can be applied to Calley as well. The evil is there but the interesting thing is, of course, Calley's case was almost programed—by his whole life's history, by the false idolatrous values of the culture, by the army training he got or failed to get, so that when he found himself in a crisis situation, this was his response. But it was a response not only to what his life-history taught him, but to the deeply irrational thrust in all of us.

When I was a very young man there was a popular song that ran, "There's a Little Bit of Bad in Every Good Little Girl, They're All the Same. Mother Eve was very very good, but even she raised Cain." It has stuck with me ever since. We have a tendency to impute these evil thrusts to cultural factors only, forgetting that they are part of our whole homonoid heritage. We have focused so hard on ecology that we have scanted ethology, with its awareness of that homonoid heritage. This is one reason for my concern about a too uncritical "social engineering" approach to society—destroying, replacing, rebuilding, as if it were only an engineering project. It isn't. It is an organism, and when the organism is ripped apart the terrible totalitarian thrust of aggressions and destructiveness within all of us gets a chance to come out.

Notes

1. Max Lerner, *America as a Civilization; Life and Thought in the United States Today* (New York: Simon and Schuster, 1957).
2. Jean François Revel, *Without Jesus or Marx* (Garden City, N.Y.: Doubleday, 1971).
3. Lewis Mumford, *Transformations of Man* (New York: Harper, 1956).

Discussion

FERKISS: I have a point I want to make here. I don't want to enter directly into the argument between Mr. Lerner and Mr. Bookchin about hierarchy and the nature of man. I have a feeling that probably Mr. Lerner is right, but we will never know until we try something different and part of our problem has been that if we assume that a certain person is going to do the right thing this is not necessarily a self-fulfilling prophesy. If we assume that he is going to do the wrong thing, it almost always is. So we really have no way of knowing whether or not human beings can live without being subject to all the kinds of passions the ethologists have been regaling us about.

My bigger problem, however, is with Mr. Bookchin on this issue of the relationship between hierarchy and scarcity. Certainly, historically, the class system has been the result of scarcity. My question, however, is whether technology is, in fact, on the eve of breaking this relationship by eliminating scarcity. I confess I am something of a Neo-Malthusian when it comes to these things. I certainly cannot see that there is technology producing to excess for anyone except a handful of middle class Americans. Even within the United States we still have problems of poverty. In the world today with three and a half billion people we have terrible problems of poverty, and when we get up to seven billion or so by the year 2000 we'll have even worse problems of poverty.

Right now there is developing an international class struggle over the environment. The United Nations has scheduled a conference in 1972 in Stockholm. I understand the Brazilian government is behind the scenes trying to torpedo this. Everyone who is concerned about the conference is worried about what the Soviet Union will do, because if the Soviet Union would consult its own interests in environmental terms, given the terrible mess they've made of their environment despite the theoretical socialism, they would be supporting us. However, there is an increasing belief that they may decide to grandstand and take the side of the developing countries and say you rich nations are trying to prevent technology because you don't want us to get our fair share. The green revolution, which is supposedly taking place in India and other countries today, making possible a breakout in terms of food and the Malthusan dilemma, is going to have some of the most horrendous repercussions on the environment that you can imagine. Now it may be that I am wrong and that Mr. Bookchin is right. These are empirical questions. A fact about which there is as yet no point disputing. But Mr. Bookchin seems to compound the argument by saying that not only is it possible to eliminate scarcity through technology, but at the same time to restore a more healthy eco-structure and better relations with our environment. I say this is even more difficult to accept.

Let me also say that there are also things that it is almost impossible for technology to bring us. Certainly, some things are finite; the amount of beach front in the United States and the world for all practical purposes, the number of people who can be at certain places at certain times which may have a unique value and so on. I submit that these things will be rationed in any kind of world. And the basis upon which you do this is going to affect tremendously the kind of social structure you have. I certainly hope I'm wrong, but if I'm not then we're really in a pickle.

BOOKCHIN: I want to answer Mr. Lerner. There's a danger of creating absolutes while opposing absolutism. There is a danger of perpetuating polarization by speaking against polarization. The buts are very important words, and I think that we have to look into them very carefully, Mr. Lerner. Look farther to your notion of the irrationality of man which you have reiterated several times. There are many different interpretations of human behavior which by no means include the idea that man is inherently irrational. Moreover, I don't always know what people mean by rationality. The American goal of efficiency is regarded as a form of rationality for example. And yet I have seen, in the name of efficiency, the most insane irrationality perpetuated in the world. There is a segment of the population, for example, located primarily around the White House lawn, which speaks about the rationality of guns and so forth. And I'm sure, that Mr. Agnew regards himself as an endlessly rational man.

Now out of all these categories, what I think we have to deal with more than anything else is necessity. Not that I think there isn't a criterion for rationality, but ours may differ profoundly, and you may regard me as most irrational and, in fact, bestial at certain times, and I may regard you in the same category. I repeat, if I am to read, for example, Wilhelm Reich, there is underlying human nature a drive for erotic love which is not a wild libido, but which promotes harmony, except where it has been buried in certain forms of society, producing a great deal of what we would call the rationality which exists today. I do not mean to hang too much of an argument on the question of human rationality or irrationality, I would rather emphasize certain necessities in situations which concern me profoundly and the tremendous flexibility of human nature, which I think lends itself to many different types of social situations and many different types of possibilities.

The main thrust of my discussion is that we are now faced with new necessities and new possibilities, not what existed in Jefferson's time or existed in Cromwell's time or existed in Pericles' time. We now have the possibility of transcending this old tradition of rationality and irrationality. And I believe that what is most rational in these new possibilities should be developed. As a libertarian, I'm not trying to force anything on anybody. Nonetheless, I do feel that we need a new point of departure and that we now need a complete transvaluation of values.

But there is a form of liberalism that tolerates too much. There is a form of liberalism, and I'm not imputing it to anyone in particular, that goes on to say for example, let us try to make do with what we have and gradually change it.

Believe me I would love that. I would love to be able to circumvent the state. But the state doesn't want to circumvent me. That's the point. The state is watching me here in this audience somewhere. It's got a tape recorder. It is keeping records, it is tapping my line, it is producing a nuisance for me, and it sends out people to visit me. I would love to circumvent the state.

I'm not arguing with Jefferson. I'm talking about a new point of departure and, in all fairness to Jefferson, I would like to say that Jefferson was also circumvented, that the Democratic party, which speaks in his name, is hardly to be conceived of as the outcome of his view or even his position. So I'm not even going to get into the issue of what ultimately comes out of a position. The thing that I would like to point out is this: I'm not denigrating technology. What I'm trying to say is that the technology that we have today is plastic and it can be reworked. Another thing I would like to say is that I do not believe that we should walk off into the forest. People who want to can do so. Again, people can do what they want to provided they don't hurt others; physically prevent them from living their own full lives.

The point that I'm emphasizing is not that we do away with cities but that we restore new communities. So that I'm not trying to say that technology should be abandoned and I'm not trying to say that communities should be abandoned, but that we have to interpret technology and community along new lines. It is necessary for us to do so. The natural world right now in a sense is telling us as best it can, that our waters are polluted, that our marine life is now faced with massive destruction, that our atmosphere is undergoing changes. This by no means can be compared with the more local type of destruction that occurred around Jefferson's time or that occurred, for that matter, around the time of Carthage or around the time of the Moslem or Barbarian invasion. We now are faced with global breakdown. We are faced with the massive fact that we can't circumvent the cities, that we can't circumvent the automobile. Talk to an auto worker in Detroit and try to get him to appreciate how he is going to circumvent the corporation. In this particular case he can't even get to his job without an automobile. He may hate the automobile. And I know of cases where workers have engaged in sabotage in automobile factories because they didn't like the motor. But they have to use automobiles, they are compelled to use automobiles. In other words, the attempt to circumvent the whole organization of society rests on a false polarity between the individual and society. If you could get around these corporations, if you could get around these states, if they would stay away, if their police powers would wither, then I would be very happy to circumvent them. But there is a polarity which you preserve in speaking against polarity, and there is an absolute which you preserve in speaking against absolutes. And that happens to be this whole lousy rotten system. Not that I think that you're committed to it. I think you don't like it, I think you're aware of its horrors, but the point that I am getting at is that, in fact, by making this type of argument, you essentially ask for what is really the impossible in the name of the rational. We have to change society. I repeat, it will have to be a change which will lead to new types of communities, not to abandon them. It will have to lead to new types of technology. And it is not something that I believe any elite in the name of revolution can force on this society. I am against elitism of any sort. I am against any type of organization which is hierarchical.

One last point about technology harmonizing. We have today almost a dozen sources of energy, ranging from solar power to wind power to geothermal energy and so on. These sources of power are not being used on any large scale today because the gigantism, the centralization, the urbanization of society on the scale that exists today makes them impractical. You cannot light up Manhattan Island with an ecology of power as it were, a variety of sources of power. But if you decentralize communities, it is now possible to create a new energy set in which many sources of energy will interplay with each other. Variety will be integrated into this organism. It will become truly an organic community, tailored for the ecosystem in which it is located. This is possible for the Third World today. The green revolution is built on our industrial principle.

What I've said about energy could be said about every aspect of life in which the integration of many variegated forms into an organic whole can be achieved. I believe this will emerge out of the most basic needs of the historical level which we have reached and it is in this sense that I say that it is a necessity. Not in any totalitarian or elitist sense.

LERNER: I'd like to make a very very brief comment on that. As we go on, I think we are clarifying where we have some common ground and where we disagree. First, about the new necessities of our time. Of course I agree. This has been true for some time in our history. One of the best statements I recall illustrating this was the message that Lincoln sent to Congress in 1862. Remember that wonderful passage: "The dogmas of the quiet past are inadequate to the stormy present. As our situation is new, so must our thinking be new and our actions be new." You couldn't have a better statement of the sense of a totally new situation. But we have had that sense of a totally new situation at a whole succession of points in American history. Not just Lincoln, but before him to Jackson, and before him and so on. Certainly Hamilton and Madison and the rest of them had that sense. And I think that this is part of the process of American history and American life. And I do not sum up American life only in terms of the giants, the monsters, the tyrannical instruments of which Mr. Bookchin speaks.

What I am saying is that in that progression, the extent to which the situation is new, the extent to which the necessities are urgent and imperative is probably greater today than at any previous period in our history. I would think also that if you looked at it in world terms, and this is a world problem, that probably there has been nothing quite comparable to the present situation since maybe the end of the Middle Ages. Paul Goodman says there hasn't been such a period of change since the time of the Reformation. My hunch is that it compares with the time when the Middle Ages moved on into a new phase. In that sense the kinds of things that we are confronting here today are radically important. But again I emphasize that we have worked out in our history a method for dealing with both crises and newness and that method is radical and even revolutionary change. And I come back to the basic proposition that I made a while ago, the revolution is upon us, we are in the midst of it. But in resolving these revolutionary changes the question is what direction do we take, how do we channel these changes. Some of the directions are destructive, others are creative. How do we channel them? We need to form some judgment between them, and that's what I mean by rational, Mr. Bookchin. I mean reflective thinking about ends and means and values.

Now man is a bundle of a number of things. One is this rationality which we have worked out painfully over the millenia; another is the non-rational which you allude to when you speak of Wilhelm Reich and love. Obviously that is the non-rational, and it is a very crucial element. Not only Reich but even Freud spoke of the struggle between eros and thanatos; the struggle between the love principle, the life principle, and the death principle. And when I spoke of what ethology has to tell us, I suppose I was rephrasing one of the things Freud was trying to say: that the death principle is in us and in society both, along with the life principle, and along with the rational. And we are a bundle of all three. And societies are a bundle of all three; but the only way in which you are going to be able to channel these revolutionary changes into constructive creative channels is by some reflective thinking.

May I say, Mr. Bookchin, I never said that you were a radical. I hope that there is a lot of the radical in you, as indeed I hope that there is some of the radical in me. I know that there is a lot of the anarchist in you, and I've tried to say that I'm trying in a small way to find some compassable units, non-governmental, non-corporate; face to face arrangements. Communities, communes, whatever they are that can be viable. I don't think that labeling of that kind is going to get us very far. I would disagree with your statement that the trouble with the liberal is that he tolerates too much. I do not tolerate the intolerable, but I do not force my own moral imperialism upon others. And if that means being a liberal, then I'm a liberal. That's what liberalism is. But I don't think these terms have very much meaning anymore. The crux is, as Holmes said, think things not words. And I think you and I and our colleagues here are all making an effort to think things. And I think it is best if we all settle on that effort. I did not speak against polarities, I spoke for them. What I said was there is an ambiguity in the human situation and the human situation is a polar situation. And society is polar. I don't know, I guess I just didn't make myself clear. But you certainly misread what I was saying.

And when you speak of interpreting technology and community along new lines, I'm completely with you. When you say we have to change society, I'm completely with you. But at that point I say we are in the midst of changing society more rapidly than it has been changed in the whole of American history right at this particular point. It is moving faster, more drastically, in terms of the counterculture, in terms of a whole series of rebellions, in terms of the efforts to narrow the gap of injustice and inequity, in terms of rethinking love and marriage and courtship, in terms of new literature, new movies, new plays, and so on. We are in the midst of a degree of social change and acceleration of social change such as we've never had. And in those terms I would suggest to you that there may not be as much difference between us as you think. I too am all in favor of changing society, but I see the perspective within which the change needs to take place in rather different terms than yours.

BOOKCHIN: I am a radical. I want to get that straightened out. I believe in very radical change in society. I believe that society is changing very rapidly. I believe that the counterculture is undergoing or producing enormous changes. Getting back again to the question of polarity, I believe that at the same time we are moving increasingly toward authoritarianism, toward repression, and as close to fascism as America has ever gotten, although I don't believe it's here yet. So what I think we are discussing here is not just abstractions like change. And the thing that disturbs me is that everything seems to come into the realm of abstraction when you talk of change. There are some changes going on now. One change is the counterculture and the other is the attempt to repress it. So the word change should not conceal the fact that we are also changing in the direction of totalitarianism. That we are not only changing, but we are racing in that direction. And that concerns me profoundly also. I won't speak at great length on other points that you've made except simply to say that I do agree that we have a great deal of differences.

3

Symposium on Technology and Authority

Seymour Melman

The relation of technology to society is a field of growing importance, but one whose literature is replete with confused ideas as to the meaning of its most elemental terms: technology and society. A mystique of technology has been developed by many writers which holds that society is not only powerfully affected by technology, but that man and society have become the creatures of the machine. Technology is understood as having its own internal dynamics and direction: man's inventing only makes concrete what is predetermined by the inherent scheme of the machine process itself. The resulting view is that men, individually and as society, are significantly shaped by the self-initiated technology.[1]

In fact, social relations, the relations of people to people, are an altogether different class of phenomena from the relation of people to things. When these two universes are confused, the characteristic results include constraints on understanding either the laws of social behavior or the nature of technology. A good place to start an analysis of these matters is with a discussion of the variability of technology.

The Ford Motor Company is one of many corporations that owns and operates factories in different countries. During the 1950s I examined aspects of production operations in the Ford factories in Detroit, U.S.A., as against those in Dagenham, outside London, England.[2] I found striking differences between Detroit and Dagenham. The factories in Detroit were using much more powered equipment for each worker. The factories at Dagenham produced similar products, but had work methods that required much more muscle power, more use of human sensory-motor capability than those in Detroit. Stated differently: there was a much higher intensity of mechanization of production work in Detroit as compared to England. The similarities among these factories included the product being the same, the company being the same, the underlying scientific knowledge in both places being the same, both places having ample staffs of engineers and ample access to technological knowledge, and both places having ample access to capital for the purpose of designing and operating production facilities. The differences in degree of mechanization remained to be explained.

I found that this variation in mechanization could be accounted for as a result of accompanying variation in the relative cost of labor to machinery in the two

49

countries. Thus in 1950 in the United States it was possible for an employer, at the cost of hiring a worker for one hour, to buy 157 kilowatt hours of electricity. In England, the employer could use the cost of employing a worker for one hour to buy only 37 kilowatt hours of electricity. Hence, employers interested in minimizing the total money cost of doing particular work were required to buy more electricity and fewer man-hours in Detroit and to buy more man-hours and less electricity in Dagenham, England.

This example illustrates two aspects of technology: first, the characteristic availability of alternatives; and second, that the design of technology is determined, within the limits of our knowledge of nature, by man's social (in this case economic) criteria.

You can begin with the simplest task, like making a hole of specified size and shape in a one inch thickness of wood. And you discover immediately that you can make that hole by a great array of methods. You can start with a blunt instrument, like a knife. You can advance to a device that has a drill bit, powered by hand, and move on to the same drill powered by a motor. Further, the same device can be held in place by a table. Beyond that there is a similar device mounted on the floor; the alternatives extend to a device that will automatically put a work piece in place, perform the drilling operation, measure it for an acceptable dimension, remove the work piece, and transfer it to a stack of finished work.

The characteristic condition of technology today is that we have a great array of alternatives for accomplishing any given task. The array of alternatives exists owing to our growing knowledge of nature and an economic interest in using that knowledge to enable work to be done with fewer man-hours. The effect is that for any work task there is no unique technology or technology option. There is an array of options.

Secondly, the variation in mechanization between the automobile factories in England and the United States has reflected the way technology in use is determined by differing social criteria within limits set by nature and the available knowledge thereof. Technology, thus, means the use of knowledge of nature to serve a social requirement. The social requirement can vary. In the auto industry example that I cited the key social requirement was an economic one: to minimize the total money costs of doing given work. That requirement dictated much labor and a little machinery in England, less labor and more machinery in the United States.

It is possible to set other requirements for technology. Thus, either in designing or selecting production equipment you can give priority to minimizing man-hours of work, or accidents to the worker, or fatigue to the worker. You can also design or select for machine durability, for reliability, for minimum maintenance requirements. A factory designed with an eye toward minimizing noise, or holding noise below the levels where it causes undesirable physical effects, will be a different factory from one that ignores that criterion.

Imagine a row of engineers, each one given a different prime criterion for designing a gasoline-engined passenger car. The first one to design it with minimum money costs of operation. The next one to design it with stress on safety for the driver. Another to design it with the main emphasis on mechanical reliability, let's say over an arbitrary period of fifteen years of use. The next, with an eye toward maximizing fuel efficiency. Another to design for minimizing vehicle contribution to air pollution. And so on.

The varying prime criteria of these design assignments will cause the engineers to produce, in each instance, a design manifestly different from the others. This illustrates how, with given knowledge of nature, the preferences of men are embodied in the design or selection of technology.

That is the process by which man's social—especially economic—relations are imprinted upon technology. It cannot be otherwise, because there is no way to make technology that is abstracted from society. Given variety in knowledge of nature, choices must be made, and criteria for choice come from man, not from nature. Thereby, technology has built into it characteristics of the given social relational system, especially the decision-making process on production. In that way criteria for decision making (relations of production) are built into the means of production. There is no way of having a means of production without that being the case. For random selection of criteria for design or selection of technology does not seem a sensible procedure. There is no socially abstracted means of production, or other technology.

It is therefore a warranted inference that technology does not, indeed cannot, determine itself. The physical and chemical properties of materials do not cause them to leap into the shape of man's artifacts. Only man, in fact, designs and shapes every particular technology. Once created and used, the given technologies have important bearing on man's life. But the point of decision to make particular use of knowledge of nature is in man, not in the options afforded by nature.

The present character of technology can be speedily appreciated with the essential points summarized above. For 200 years the criteria of businessmen have dominated the design and selection of technology. During the 1950s and 1960s half and more of the research and development engineers and scientists of the United States functioned on behalf of the Department of Defense, NASA, the Atomic Energy Commission, and related agencies. Behold the technology they produced: it is, of course, tailor-made to suit the requirements of these agencies. But so important have these technologies become in the total American "new technology" output since World War II, that the military and related aerospace technologies have seemed to dominate the field and to represent technology as a whole.

Once technology is viewed as an undifferentiated whole and is evaluated with abstraction from the criteria that determine particular selections of design among alternatives, then one result is the science-fiction or political-polemical literature on Man as the Prisoner of the Machine. In this view the evil agency is not particular machines designed by engineers to suit the particular requirements of the military or business establishment, but *The Machine* in general. Actually, there is no machine in general. It is possible to make, see, touch, or observe particular machines only. When these methodological cues are translated into procedure in inquiry then one arrives, swiftly, at the appreciation that each machine has built into it the particular requirement of whoever decides its characteristics and the uses it must serve. Hence, the technology of war-making is only one among an immense array of possible aircraft technologies.

It is not surprising, however, that military technology should have had an overwhelming emotional effect on man's recent perceptions of technology and his feelings about it. Consider that military technology now makes possible an effect previously unknown in human experience: the termination of human community through willful or accidental use of nuclear weapons. I don't find it unreasonable that many sensitive people, especially among the young, should experience fearful feelings about the prospect of "no future" and that special fear should attach to the well-advertised technologies of mass destruction. The location of decision, however, is not in the missiles, but in the men who order their construction and control their use.

When the characteristics of technology are discussed in abstraction from the social processes that selectively determine them, then—apart from intention—a distortion of understanding is produced. Technology is made to appear as though independent of man's will as expressed through the selective preferences of the designing process. Or, if socially-determined design is not excluded, then the social criteria are made to appear to be without alternatives. If what is desired is a perspective of alternative possible technologies, or alternatives in decision making on production, then it is essential to focus directly on alternatives for organizing economy and society; alternatives for man's relation to man. For the social rules of man's relation to man include the social preferences (criteria) which selectively determine technology.

For some time there has been more confused discussion about technology than serious discussion about social alternatives. The neglected topics include the following: can man make decisions on production without an occupational separation between decision making and doing the work? In other words, can decisions on production be made in cooperative and democratic ways rather than by managerial-hierarchical methods? Are there conceivable, workable alternatives to features of economy and society that are basic to capitalism—whether private or statist? There is substantial evidence pointing to alternative social forms, as in the development of decision making among industrial workers, and the cooperative decision making of the kibbutz. A considerable literature describes the existence of a decision-making process among industrial workers that incorporates mutuality and democratic, nonhierarchical social forms as an operating pattern at the point of production. This workers' decision process operates and evolves in parallel with the decision process of management within industrial capitalism.[3]

The viability and efficiency of cooperative organizations in production and other areas of life is demonstrated by the Israeli kibbutz. Now into four generations, 200 kibbutzim operate highly mechanized agriculture and manufacturing industries. The main money-valued product of the kibbutz is now industrial. I recently completed an industrial study comparing efficiency under cooperative versus managerial decision making, which included six sets of cooperative versus six sets of managerial enterprises, matched in terms of products produced. The cooperatively controlled enterprises, as a group, showed as high or higher productivity of labor and capital as the managerially controlled enterprises.[4] That was not an expected result, based upon the textbook wisdom on the economics of industrial capitalism.

J. Ellul writes, in *The Technological Society*, "Capitalism did not create our world; the machine did." Following that lead, the reader who wants to explain or alter one or another aspect of "our world" is directed to *The Machine* as the prime cause of things as they are. However, neither Ellul nor the other writers on machine mysticism offer much advice on workable ways of getting *The Machine* to change "our world" in desired ways. How can we appeal to *The Machine* to do something for us? The machine mystics—if taken seriously—leave us feeling helpless, deficient in understanding, and without a guide to how to get anything done. That is the main social function of this literature. Therein lies its thrust as a status-quo conserving body of thought. Ellul's instruction that "Capitalism did not create our world; the machine did" is preceded by the admonition: "It's useless to rail against capitalism."[5]

Once *The Machine* is viewed as an all-powerful (while unexplained) source of initiative in society, then the machine-using society is endowed with characteristics whose perception requires deep knowledge of science. At the same time public affairs (politics) are made unintelligible to the ordinary man. Says Gabor:

The "modern industrial state" or the "technetronic society," as it has been variously called, is indeed above the head of the man in the street. How could the simple man decide with his vote a question, such as was put by Bertrand de Jouvenel: "How to maintain full employment, not more than 2 percent inflation per annum, and a good balance of international payments at a steady rate of real growth of not less than 3.5 percent?"[6]

The whole matter takes another form, however, if the question to the electorate is: do you favor or oppose efforts by government to ensure "full" employment, defined as no more than 2 percent unemployment? People can consider and vote on that issue, leaving the details to specialists; isn't that what we pay them for? Most people are competent to choose national priorities, preferred characteristics of consumer goods, acceptable levels of air pollution, etc. The function of specialists includes spelling out the consequences of alternatives and being responsible for designing and executing the tasks to be performed.

The theories of the machine mystique have the common quality of instructing the unwary reader on the powerlessness of man, and rationalizing the continued decision-making power of those who wield power today. Consider the important technology issue: should public atomic energy policies press on with the construction of radiation waste-producing fission reactors or try to accelerate the development of no-radiation by-product fusion processes?

The policy of the U.S. Atomic Energy Commission pushes the construction of hazardous fission reactors for power production, while giving low money priority to fusion process development. This is related to the A.E.C.'s and private corporate investments in fission technology. Until this writing the A.E.C. has given less importance to the dangerous collateral effects from major fission reactors operation. This is an economic choice with associated social value preferences. That choice is in no conceivable sense initiated or determined by technology. Here is a major choice among alternative technologies that is clearly determined by social, specifically economic, criteria.

The writers on the machine mystique, independently of intention, imply a prescription to be obedient to the Atomic Energy Commission and others who now make decisions on the nature of technology and its uses. On the other hand, simply being rebellious in a random way is not relevant. It is important to know that alternatives are conceivable in technology, and that the key causal factor is not in nature or in technology itself, but consists of man's social relations which give the instruction as to the kind of technologies that are made and used.

Therefore the issue is not *The Machine*, for or against, but rather: what alternatives are conceivable and possible in social relations and collateral technology, and how preferred alternatives can be realized.

Notes

1. Z. Brzezinski, *Between Two Ages: America's Role in the Technetronic Era* (Viking, 1970); J. Ellul, *The Technological Society* (Vintage Books, 1964); D. Gabor, *Innovations: Scientific, Technological, and Social* (Oxford University Press, 1970); L. Mumford, *The Myth of the Machine: The Pentagon of Power*, Vol. 2 (Harcourt, Brace, Jovanovich, 1967-1970).

2. Seymour Melman, *Dynamic Factors in Industrial Productivity* (Oxford: Basil Blackwell, 1956).

3. Seymour Melman, *Decision-Making and Productivity* (Oxford: Basil Blackwell, 1958).

4. Seymour Melman, "Managerial Versus Cooperative Decision Making in Israel," *Studies in Comparative International Development*, Vol. VI, 1970-1971, No. 3 (New Brunswick, New Jersey: Rutgers University).

5. Ellul, *The Technological Society.*

6. Gabor, *Innovations.*

Melvin M. Tumin

I find, as I'm sure all of you do, that Dr. Melman's remarks are a very salutary and welcome counter-balance to Mr. Mumford's eloquent metaphorizing of the menace of the megamachine. Withal, I also find Dr. Melman lacking a little bit of mysticism. For he has neglected to reflect that experience all of us have had with the apparent demonic nature of machines, which seem to develop their own autonomy, and then exhibit a stubborn recalcitrance to any human attempt at control. If you've ever dealt with a washing machine that turns itself on when *it* wishes to, you know what I mean.

More seriously, now, if one is to remain somewhere within one standard deviation of sanity, one ought to distinguish between the relations of man to things and the relations of man to man. There has emerged in the modern epoch a new kind of animism or animitism, analogous to primitive man's identification of man and nature, such that we invest what we find in the world of nature with human qualities and, reciprocally, we conceive of man in terms of the qualities we find in nature. In the same vein, there are many today who are treated by their "rulers" (in government, corporations, and universities) as though they were things, while machines are deferred to and respected as though they were men.

The thingification of man and the anthropomorphization of machines are characteristics of an approach to technology that suggests that while all technology is, in principle, subject to man's controls, we often act as if once a machine is in movement, the power reverses so that machines then exercise a determinate influence upon us. This renunciation of power and ascription of autonomy to machines naturally leads to the most dour pessimism. On the other hand, it is claimed that it is man who both puts in the plug that starts the machines, and can always pull out the plug to stop the machines, making it possible to maintain a sense of optimism about the human situation.

This contrast between optimism and pessimism also distinguishes Dr. Melman's general approach from Mr. Mumford's. They obviously prefer two quite different ways in which to view the world. I don't want to equate Dr. Melman with a Victorian novelist, nor Mr. Mumford with one of the world's distinguished writers, but I see Mr. Mumford as saying, along with Goethe, that "Viewed from the heights of reason all life looks like some malignant disease and the world like a madhouse," while Dr. Melman strikes me as more affiliated with Anthony Trollope, who has one of his characters say, in the *Eustace Diamonds*, that "a huge, daily, living, increasing grievance that does one no palpable harm is the happiest possession that a man can have." In considering these matters. I admonish you that I am likely to end up on the side of Trollope and Melman.

There are three main questions that the title of the talks suggest we should address ourselves to.

First, Can man get control over his technology? I think that Dr. Melman has answered that for us, as well as could possibly be done within the time allotted to him.

The second question is, Can this society (call it modified capitalism, proto-capitalism, neo-capitalism, post-capitalism, or whatever), with its capitalist economic orientations and its democratic political structures, solve certain fundamental pressing problems within its present boundaries and forms, or is a basic reorganization of society required?

Third, in order to bridge over to the symposium on counterculture, I want to ask, Can human consciousness be recreated to initiate, propel, and institutionalize new and desired forms of relationships between man and his environment and man and other men?

This last question is crucial because, if it is true, as I along with Dr. Melman believe it is, that it is fundamentally man's world to make and create and recreate as he sees fit, then the question of the role of new consciousness in that creation becomes central.

(It is curious that the question of consciousness should have become so prominent just at a time when it appears as though the power to structure the basic institutional relationships is out of the hands of the majority of the people. It seems almost as if the Marxist notion that the material conditions of history determine existing consciousness has been stood on its head, *in the name of Marx*, just as the insistence that the university is a crucial social institution, instead of a pale reflection of the economy, also stands Marx on his head.)

Now let me indicate some positions I think important in these issues:

The first is that there is no dynamism or directionality in technology per se. Consider in this regard the following crude diagram.

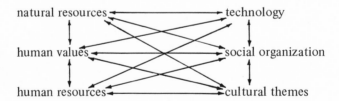

Visualize the relations among these factors as being indicated by a series of two-way arrows that connect each variable with all others, so that we have a model of a field of forces that are simultaneously compendent. Note that the major forces at work on each other here include the non-human resources in the external environment, the human resources, technology, cultural themes and styles, social organization, and human values.

Since all the arrows go from everything to everything else, this suggests a flow of forces such that one can start at any point in the circle and trace influences emanating from that one variable upon all others. So conceived, technology is seen as having a force of its own, but this is immediately modified by realizing that such force as it has is acquired from the operations of human decisions and power structures and the remaining variables. This model illustrates what we mean when we say there is no power or direction in technology itself.

Second, slogans will not do and emoting will not do if we're going to deal seriously with problems of man and technology. It may be understandable why some people behave irrationally, out of despair. But strong feeling is no substitute for rational analysis. If one is interested in getting some comprehension of the complexity of this problem, one must take the emotional outbreaks and the understandable despairs of many people with the conditions of their lives as elements in the field that one has to analyze. But they are no substitute for analysis.

Third, stereotypes won't do when we are looking for rational solutions. Not stereotypes of age, nor of sex, nor of class, because there are no categories of people who are excluded from possible contributions to sensible and concerned solutions to the problem. It is always theoretically possible to transcend the parochial limits of one's "vested interests" and to arrive at judgments and values that are *not* consonant with some narrow calculation of such self-interest. So, no stereotypes about position and social structure, please, nor any slogans such as "science won't save us" or "science will save us." Of course, if one identifies rationality with science, then, if science won't save us, nothing else will. But I also recognize that science by itself never saved anything. For science is like technology: it is an instrument that man can use as he sees fit. It has certain rules, and if you play by them, you get certain gains, and if you don't play by them, you don't get the gains. When you want to do something other than science, do that, but don't call that the same as science. Thus, if you want to talk about poetry, intuition, and feeling, those are experiences that have importance in some aspects of our lives, but they are not a substitute for science. On the other hand, science is not a substitute for love either. But love won't save us either. So, I take it for granted that it is possible to transcend over one's origins.

You, the students at this conference, as a group are the best evidence in support of that premise. For you have every vested interest in the world in just shutting up, minding your own business, wearing your hair short, being neatly dressed, and going about making your way in this world. You're going to "make it," because you're a privileged elite. Yet, ironically, you have chosen, many of you at least, to transcend over the greatest difficulty, namely, that of class *advantage*. One can understand transcending over disadvantages. But transcending over an *advantaged* position is a much more difficult thing to do. You are a living example of such transcendence over advantage. One must really wonder how can people like you seriously pose yourselves the question of how you can best go about subverting the privileges you are now enjoying. For that, in some sense, is the *ideological* charge of this meeting. So, one asks, what are the circumstances by which you came into this "false consciousness?" Then one goes on to ask whether it may be possible for others, too, to transcend their social positions and arrive at points of view that deviate from the normative expectations of their own narrowly defined social positions.

Fourth, I want also to urge that arguments about the "system" causing things, which confine themselves to global denunciations of *the* system, are as meaningless as all stereotypes about women, blacks, Jews, university people, and age-groups. For *the* system is a multi-factored thing. It has many dimensions to it; it has great irregularities; it has a number of competing ideologies running through it. There are various irregular degrees of freedom in the differing institutional networks. Hence, to put the choice as one between free will or total determinism by *the* system seems to me both silly and immoral because it leads then to an acceptance either of total responsibility for what we do in life or total lack of responsibility. There is too much institutional molding of choices, on the one hand, and too much open avenues of choice on the other, to accept either of those versions.

Fifth, I would argue that alterations of society that take the form of changing the ownership of the instruments for production are not *sufficient* conditions for a new quality of life, or for a new relationship between man and technology. They may or may not even be *necessary* conditions, depending on which change you're seeking. No one in his right mind would contend that the Soviet Union which has eliminated private ownership of the instruments of production has thereby eliminated everything that goes along with the evils of capitalism. It has not only retained some of the evils of capitalism and some of the remaining evils of czarism, but it has invented many of its own. I repeat, then, that change in the formal structure of ownership of the instruments of production is not a *sufficient* condition and may not even be a necessary condition for basic changes in the quality of life. Much depends on what changes you want, and at what cost, and how quickly, and how sure you are that you're going to get there.

Sixth, I would argue that the ends never justify the means, nor vice versa. Rather, with John Dewey, I would assert that the sum total of all the means that you engage in along the way to an end constitute the end that you achieve. Everything you do along the way represents what you have achieved at any stopping point. They represent your life, and *your* effects upon you, and your effects upon others, and the cumulation of all that is the end you have achieved. This version of means-ends is very different from that which argues either that the ends justify the means or the means justify the ends.

I have deliberately taken the time to state these positions on diverse issues concerning social behavior because they seem to me to be necessary cautionaries in thinking about the problem of technology-in-society. That problem has been posed hyper-dramatically, of course, by asking whether technology will come to rule us, unless we do away with it. The implication for some is that we can do away with our modern technological society and return to some form of agricultural communal life. But this is patent nonsense. For the simple fact is that even if we were at zero population growth, our present world population cannot conceivably be sustained, on even a minimal level of decency, without a vast multiplication of technology applied to all forms of life-sustaining activities.

It follows, too, that such a technological multiplication could not conceivably be organized with any degree of efficiency without proliferating bureaucratic structures apposite to them. One can hope, of course, that we have learned enough about how bureaucratic and technocratic structures come to assume a certain malign autonomy. But I repeat we cannot manage even to feed today's world without large-scale technology and bureaucracy. It will not pay, therefore, to make "demons" out of them, investing them with their own life and dynamics, and treating them as though they were reified forces beyond our control. Both technology and bureaucracy are man-made instruments. Without them we should still be trying to feed billions of people with digging-stick technologies and town-hall or tribal-council, social-organizational structures, and obviously failing.

Our own society's enormous growth and development has unquestionably been due in significant part to technological and bureaucratic efficiency, but also to two main value systems, among others, that have nourished us. One has been an almost unconquerable belief in an ever-upward spiralling of "progress," marked mostly by growth in material productivity. The other has been a continuous commitment, in both values and action, to the idea of a political democracy. One can take account of all our shortcomings and inadequacies as a democratic society, and one can express many reservations and doubts about the "progress" of the last fifty years. But the fact remains incontestable that because we have collectively adopted an optimistic mood about ever-higher standards of well-being, and because we have been a politically self-correcting society, we have managed to survive relatively intact through major crises that have torn other societies asunder.

Now, however, we face an epoch during which serious voices of doubt are being raised about what all the "progess" and "democracy" add up to. The most poignant and pointed doubts have been expressed in terms of concerns for the "quality of life" that has been generated in this society, in the midst of all its affluence. We are being asked whether we can sensibly talk about progress and democracy in view of the extant problems of war, racism, poverty, the inequality of women, and the pollution of the environment.

The seriousness and relevance of these doubts are unmistakable. Many, however, seem puzzled by the apparent suddenness with which these doubts have come to occupy the attention especially of thoughtful young people on college campuses throughout the country. I believe it important, therefore, to look into these concerns, to see the ideological sources from which they flow, and thereby to determine the extent to which they are simply momentary impulses or whether, contrariwise, they have some firm rooting in well-established modes of consciousness. It is, after all, a new consciousness, that brings the concerns about the "quality of life" to the forefront of public attention.

As I understand this consciousness, it is rooted in five major ideological mainstreams that have come to a point of convergence in the modern period, but that have for some decades now been forming the life-orientations of several generations.

There is, first, "existentialism," with its emphasis upon the idea that man invests his life with whatever meaning it may have. This stand is solidly opposed to prior notions that there is a meaning to history or to the Universe that can be discovered. The current notion denies such inherent purpose and calls attention instead to the "neutrality" of events until men invest them with meaning and purpose. This being so, it follows that the meaning of any individual's life is given by the actions he takes, and that he is the main beneficiary or victim of such "meanings" as they accrue through the consequences of his action. From this it then follows that individual autonomy in the determination of one's way of life is an imperative. As you recognize, this runs directly counter to any notions of the legitimacy of bureaucratic structures of authority or any attempt to "impose" a way of life on others. Such a stand is of course inherently inimical both to adequate functioning in a bureaucracy and to subservient roles in any established form of governance, such as is found on most college campuses.

The right to autonomy and self-determination that seems to follow from an existentialist stand is supported by the conclusions drawn from the doctrines of moral and cultural relativism, which constitute the second major ideological wellsprings of this new consciousness. The philosophers and social scientists of the twentieth century who have given currency and credence to the doctrines of moral and cultural relativism have by that act also given support to the claim by many, especially among the college educated, that there are no absolute criteria for measuring value or worth and that the final condition of man is one in which he must take his stands, arbitrary though they may seem, since there is no final authority on moral issues to which one can appeal. Such a posture toward moral problems obviously denies the moral authority of the parental generation, or of established "governors" of institutions, and gives to the young people of today a firm sense of their right to make important moral decisions for themselves, unhindered by any considerations of tradition or of institutions such as churches that claim authority in moral questions. The spirit of individual self-determination and of freedom to revise moral codes, even drastically, that is set in motion by such moral relativism obviously is inimical to the conduct of the affairs of most traditional families, industries, and universities. This same "relativism" of morals leads to a great unwillingness on the part of many young people to engage in any moral chastisement or any effort to sanction the "different" morals of other people.

The third major ideological mainstream is identified with Marxism. From it two main ideas flow that have been extremely important in shaping the consciousness of college students today. One of these is the notion that the "system," i.e., the society and its impersonal structures and institutions, is chiefly responsible for the major lines of fate of the members of the society, so that the unfortunate are seen as "victims" of the system rather than, as traditionally, as lazy, shiftless people of low character and will. It follows, moreover, that if the system is responsible for the evils as well as the benefits that we experience today, the system must be rectified or drastically altered or, in the extreme case, "overthrown," if the symptomatic disorders of that system are to be reduced or eliminated. The radicalization of the politics of some college students derives in large part from this view of "system responsibility." So, too, does their outpouring of sympathy for and identification with the "victims," such as the poor and the blacks.

From Marxism also comes the notion of the moral propriety of an egalitarian society, one that would presumably not tolerate a large belt of poverty at the bottom of the superstructure of affluence. Since the "surplus wealth" of the society is created, according to Marxism, by the value added by workers, that surplus value, or profit, belongs to them, and not to the entrepreneurs. Hence, by these lights, corporations based on profit making are essentially immoral, as are organizations, such as universities, that thrive on the income earned from corporate investments. Some of the sense of "righteousness" in attacking universities as key institutions of a "corporate society" may be seen in these Marxist views, assuming of course that one takes them as one's basic premises.

A fourth major source of ideological inspiration derives from the work of Sigmund Freud. Though many students have never read Freud, they have been raised to be aware of the evils of repression, especially of sexual repression, and that has given them justification for new attitudes about and actual behavior in sexual relations that seem startling to an older generation. Many students have acquired these "modern" sexual orientations from their parents, at least ideologically. But the parental generation has never felt free to speak them loudly and certainly not to act them out. What we are now seeing is a young generation that is acting out the verbal precepts of its parents and causing everyone serious discomfiture thereby.

From Freud, too, however, has come the notion of the requirement of repression that civilization makes upon the instinctual energies and drives of the human being. If civilization requires repression, one may ask how much repression is worth how much civilization? Such questions are being asked in serious and often active ways by young people today.

Finally, we have had our modern minds shaped by the writings of John Dewey, not only with regard to the content of a genuinely progressive education but, just as importantly, with regard to the idea that underlies "progressive education," namely, the idea that every individual is a unique being, whose personally and socially valuable talents and dimensions have as much right to be discovered and brought into effective action as those of any other person. The doctrine of the equal uniqueness and equal rights of all people provides a solid support for both a fundamental democracy and egalitarianism.

One of the ironies of the emerging mode of consciousness is that these five main ideological streams that feed it and, in fact, constitute it, have been absorbed by many of the younger generation without any conscious awareness of the process. However, this does not make the content of these idea systems any the less effective, nor does it demean those who act in terms of them, even though they do not know by what they have been inspired to think and feel as they do.

It is also true, of course, and important to note as well, that these new doctrines have taken hold mostly of the minds of college youth, and particularly of that segment of college youth that is in some ways the most advantaged sector of youth in all important regards. But this is no accident. For the college campus is a place that has traditionally provided leisure and luxury for the contemplation of new ideas. It has provided political sanctuary from the consequences of acting on these new notions, however offensive they may be found by an outside world. It has offered any individual student an immediate company of like-minded peers to sustain him during moments when his emerging new commitments might otherwise falter. It has provided an environment that emphasizes the rightness of serious intellectual criticism of existing institutions, and has thereby engendered the spirit of dissent.

The campus is also a place typically populated by people who, as yet, have no hostages to fate and fortune, in the form of wives and children and jobs, that might be imperilled by their resolute pursuit of dissenting ideas and themes of life. Hence, it provides an ideal environment for the incubation and the preliminary trying out of new ideas and forms of social behavior, and makes it more possible, in a microscopic way, for students to bring their actual behavior into much closer conformity with their ideal values than would be true in the outside world. Knowing all these felicitous supporting features of the college campus, one may indeed cherish that environment as a treasure in the house of human liberty and self-development. At the same time, one must unhappily recognize that it is an extraordinarily deviant and privileged environment, as compared with any other.

Knowing, then, the extent to which these new ideas and the consciousness they constitute have come to command your attention and often your fealty, the question is whether these same ideas and consciousness might come to be disseminated more widely to people living in quite different and much less supportive environments.

Assuming for the moment the high probability that there are not any other comparably felicitous environments, we have to ask whether there are function-ally-equivalent situations in life outside of college campuses that might serve the same purposes. Can people at lower levels of fortune "rise" to this new consciousness? Can young people off college campuses, and without the edge on fortune that a college education provides, come to see the world in the same way? Can others who have not yet experienced affluence, leisure, and luxury come to see and worry about the negative features of the affluent life that seem to animate your concerns so much? Can others who have not yet begun to enjoy the benefits of modern technology and efficient, bureaucratic organization of production come to disdain these as you are now doing?

Probably, very probably the answer to all these questions is "No." Very probably these other populations will first have to have the opportunity to enjoy a life of well-being such as you now lead before they can begin to raise questions about the balance between its costs and benefits. Very probably, too, these other cohorts of our society, and of other societies, will have to experience the fullness of material gratifications before they can come to feel the hollowness of things about which you complain.

If, therefore, you come to feel that you are a small island of persons with heightened consciousness, in the midst of a sea of people who are just beginning to enjoy a portion of that which you now ideologically disdain, you must understand this, as good historical materialists, as just what one might expect, given the doctrine that existence shapes consciousness. Nor would it be gracious or historically moral to sit in condemnation of the many others who have not yet come to experience the benefits of advanced modern technology and wealth.

Yet one may properly ask whether it may not be possible for future cohorts of young men and women to condense the time that might otherwise be required, in a normal social-evolutionary cycle, to rise to the awareness of the concept of "the quality of life," which you have come to pose so vigorously against those who blandly measure our well-being alone by our gross national product. Perhaps it is not unthinkable that future generations may experience a form of "combined development," so that they may sustain high levels of material well-being, at the same time that they do not pay as many prices in the deteriorated quality of life about which this conference has expressed so much concern.

In the interim, it is vital for all those concerned about the egregious impact of the technological society on the quality of life, to realize that this new consciousness, focussing on life's qualities as it does, is a powerful and now deeply-rooted social weapon. Its power arises from a number of important sources.

First, it has a shock value, for it so directly and contrarily confronts established placid attitudes that revolve around the GNP as the measure of well-being.

Second, it is able to prolong the impact, after the initial shock, because it is so highly suffused with moral tones that even the GNP fans cannot easily avoid. Evoking human concern for human well-being, as it does, over a wide spectrum of human values and modalities, it is obviously a more generous and comprehensive view of man than that contained in the GNP perspective. Moreover, it has the power of the traditional appeal to the spiritual and humanistic values in human life as opposed to the more narrow appeal to the material gratifications. It may be curious that a group of young people who are, on the average, more Marxist-minded than most, should seem to be reversing the traditional order of things. But that is the case.

Third, this consciousness commands power because it is the vision of young people who have long lives to lead, and who will, in the normal course of events, come to take up positions of leadership in this society. They may not retain the *fullness* of their youthful visions along the road to social and political power. But it is predictable that a substantial margin of the vision that now animates such young people is likely to find itself expressed in the concrete policies and laws that these young people will come to formulate, advocate, and institutional-ize when they acquire their adult power positions.

Fourth, this consciousness is more powerful than it might otherwise be simply because it represents a distillation of the ideological convictions of a number of the members of the older generation who are, by that token, disarmed from any effective or strong opposition to its advocacy. In this light, it must be remembered that it was the parents of the present generation of college students who were first exposed and who first came to embrace, albeit gingerly, the doctrines of existentialism, moral and cultural relativism, Marxism, Freudian-ism, and the insights of John Dewey.

This is no vapid, ethereal vision, then; this new consciousness. There is nothing about it that is quite so feathery as is implied in the "Greening of America." Quite to the contrary. It is toughminded; it has fundamental conceptions of the nature of man underlying it; it has an immanently moral core; it has durability; and it can be implemented in social institutional practices over time. It represents an attitude toward the relationship between man and machines that, once stripped of romantic exaggerations and self-destroying excesses, can serve as a powerful set of overarching values, that may indeed restore some sane balance among the many human needs and values that are competing for realization today. If the spirit that summoned this conference into being can persist, as there is every good reason to believe it can, there is also every good reason to assume that in the next two decades we shall see a significant reassertion of man's ability to control his own fate, and to adopt his own created technology to his own values.

It is crucial, finally, that all this transpire within the framework of a self-correcting polity, namely, democracy. Only as we sustain the basic processes of political self-correction and do not, out of despair, cry for the destruction of all things, as though by some magic there will then be human renewal, can we hope to implement the vision contained in this new consciousness.

E. Digby Baltzell

I would like to elaborate on some of the ideas raised by the two previous speakers. I was particularly interested in Mr. Melman's remarks about his study of the two factories, one in Detroit and the other in England. I would assume that the fact that one can purchase some 200 kilowatts of electric power for the price of one worker in America, as against only 50 kilowatts per British worker, is at least partly a reflection of the less technocratic, and more humanistic, values of the British as compared with ourselves.

This, of course, raises the immediate question: why the contrasting values held by these two great industrial cultures? Before suggesting any answers to this question, let me make some further observations on the contrasting values of these two cultures. In his book, *The End of Ideology*,[1] Daniel Bell gave us two different responses to similar situations. On the one hand, Bell observed that a turnpike was being routed down through New England to New York City; the most *technically* efficient route would have gone right through the center of an historic cemetery where some very distinguished Americans were buried. At about the same time in England, a new turnpike (still, by the way, referred to as a "carriageway") was being built out of London; the most *technically* efficient route would have gone through an historic Gothic arch which was too small to allow large modern buses and lorries to pass under it. As might be expected, the leaders of the two cultures made quite different decisions: In New England, the ancient graves were ripped up and the turnpike routed in the most technically efficient straight line; in Old England, the turnpike was routed around the ancient arch, tradition and historic continuity having triumphed over purely technical considerations, humane logic triumphed over technical logic.

One can find many many other examples of the contrasts between the values of these two cultures. In a recent trip through England, for example, I kept asking myself why there were so few ugly telephone poles and wires cluttering up the beautiful countryside as in America? I discovered this was because they place them underground. Why no endless strip development and second-hand car lots which blight the outskirts of almost every town in America? Simply because the English leadership does not allow it and has instituted zoning laws against such consumate ugliness.

Our modern civilization, of course, is based on the automobile and various other means of rapid movement and communication. Telephone wires, turnpikes, and automobiles are here to stay. It is not a matter of doing away with them in the Luddite tradition; rather we must make them our servants rather than our masters.

There is, I think, a long tradition in America which has produced the particular set of values which include technology as master rather than as means. It undoubtedly has something to do with our well-known cult of efficiency, which is quite naturally the enemy of tradition. One recalls the brilliant and iconoclastic writings of Thorsten Veblen, who loved to ridicule the reactionary peculiarities of all sorts of "leisure-class" traditions which were forever holding us back from pursuing pure functional (or technical) efficiency. It was no wonder that Veblen was one of the patron saints of the "gray-suited" and "gray car" *Technocracy* Movement. Or take the case of the term "culture-lag," one of the more famous concepts in the jargon of American sociology, coined by William F. Ogburn in his book *Social Change.*[2] Like Veblen, and like Marx, Ogburn's term meant that the normative culture (or superstructure) had a reactionary way of lagging behind the rapid changes in technological efficiency, and technological progress. But why, we ought to be asking ourselves today, should cultural values chase after technological advances (innovations) rather than bending and shaping (or not even using) the technology to suit our traditional cultural values or social and political forms? Have the British necessarily "lagged" behind us just because they prefer the traditional drafty halls and open fireplaces to the central heating (and overheating) which is now considered a necessity for all Americans, from Maine to Florida, from the home of the slum-dweller to the millionaire's mansion?

What I have been trying to suggest, following Mr. Melman, is that British cultural values seem to include a more humanistic and less technocratic basis for making decisions than has been the case in America. I would further like to suggest the possibility that these contrasting sets of values are related to the different attitudes towards hierarchy and authority in these two cultures.

On the one hand, the English value system has been firmly and traditionally anchored in a strong sense of *deference* to a hegemonic set of upperclass values which include, among other things, (1) a sense of amateurism rather than professionalism, (2) an emphasis on stability rather than change, and (3) a general, classical or humanistic, rather than technical or scientific, education—at least for the sons of upper class members.

Our American values, on the other hand, are certainly not based on any deference to upper class authority; on the contrary, as foreign observers from Harriet Martineau and Tocqueville to James Bryse have found out, egalitarian ideals and disrespect for hierarchical authority have had a long tradition in this country. In contrast to the British, our values are to be found in the middle class ethic of mobility and change, in the values of the professional expert rather than the gentleman amateur, and in science rather than the humanities.

Now, of course, the difference in values between the two countries is not a matter of kind, but degree. The deference or hierarchical set of values, for instance, are held in higher regard in the older communities along the eastern seaboard (and in the Old South in particular) than in the newer communities in the West, which are more geared towards the middle class values of mobility, equality, and change. The acceptance of sociology (in many ways an excellent index of the acceptance of a technical, scientist and perhaps even dehumaniz-ing view of man) was, for instance, much more rapid in the Middle West than in the eastern part of this country. In England, as might be expected, it was taken up by the newer, "Red Brick" universities rather than by the upper class strongholds at "Oxbridge." Following the same logic, both in England and America, sociologists have been far more likely to have originated in the lower-middle and lower classes than, for example, historians or students of literature and the arts. Nor is it any accident that these practicing sociologists who take a humanistic approach to their discipline are often called "soft" and, thus, suspect (especially in America), while those who model their work on the natural sciences are called "hard" and, thus, good (for grants, at least, from both the government and the private foundations). Moreover, from a more inclusive point of view, is it not true that science and engineering, in both countries, tend to be middle rather than upper class vocations? The College of the City of New York, for instance, has produced far more graduates who have gone on to achieve Ph.D.'s in chemistry, physics, and engineering than have the graduates of Harvard College.

Now all of us, being all too human, are subject to the occupational hazard which Veblen nicely called "trained incapacity." Every profession or craft trains us to see in a certain way, to see things from a particular point of view, and thus, inadvertently due to our training, to fail to take other points of view into account. That is to say, the poet is likely to take a poetic view of the world and, at the same time, is likely to be blind to the point of view which sees tears of sorrow as merely H_2O following the laws of gravity. All of us have our point of view as well as our blind spots: psychologists are prone to psychologism, sociologists to sociologism and scientists to scientism. Which is to say we all are subject to the vices of our virtues, or the temptation to make legitimate means into ends. The poet or the philosopher is far more likely to see this sorry world as tragic veil of tears, while his more scientifically-oriented friend may see it as a splendid opportunity for more perfect social engineering, dictatorship and violence eventually being abolished by the compulsory psychoanalysis of all candidates for leadership positions. Few of them would have read, or taken to heart, the great European humanist, Ignazio Silone's book *The School for Dictators*,[3] which shows how the values of a naive, American sociologist are, perhaps, just the ones which have led to the flight of freedom from our modern, disenchanted world.

What I am trying to suggest here is the simple proposition that a culture or subculture dominated by a middle class, scientistic, and technical set of values will be more likely to lead perfectly honorable and intelligent men into the trap of technocracy or scientism than would be the case of a culture where men still cling to upper class, hierarchical, and humanistic values. Again, it is not a matter of either/or, but of degree, more or less. In our society the scientistic subculture is more dominant than has been the case with England. And just as the former values led to ripping up the graveyard and the latter to routing 'round the arch, so one would predict that we would be more likely to make efficiency an end in itself rather than one factor in attaining more humanistic ends; to make the surgeon's knife, the psychiatrist's couch, the sociologist's survey, as well as the pill and the automobile, our masters rather than our servants.

Notes

1. Daniel Bell, *End of Ideology* (Glencoe: Free Press, 1960).
2. William F. Ogburn, *Social Change With Respect to Culture and Original Nature*, 2nd edition (New York: Viking, 1950).
3. Ignazio Silone, *School for Dictators* (New York: Harper, 1938).

Discussion

AUDIENCE: Have you not overlooked the main point of Jacques Ellul's book, *The Technological Society?*

MELMAN: I haven't overlooked it. I have in fact dealt with it. The underlying matter is quite straightforward. Inanimate things do not direct themselves. The specific character of our artifacts, which we call technology, are given entirely by man-made social requirements applied to using the knowledge of nature. There's nothing in the nature of the category "tape recorder" that yields the present design. This design comes from setting as first criterion producing a serviceable machine, serviceable let's say for a period of about ten years, at a given level of maintenance, at a price that will attract a market of a calculated size. Now it's quite possible to make a tape recorder, and they are made, without regard to price, but with certain considerations of reliability which will necessarily then cost about ten times the present machine and hence have a much smaller market. I will give you further examples. An electrocardiograph was ordered designed for the flight of Colonel Glenn, the first American astronaut. When the machine was done with its function the men who did the work thought they would try to attract the attention of the medical profession. They boxed it in an available olive drab sturdy container and took it to a cardiologist. The machine was demonstrated and the cardiologist found it immensely interesting. It gave a lot of information that the ordinary electro-cardiograph didn't give. Then the cardiologist asked how much does this cost. And the answer was $6,000. Well the ordinary competent electrocardiograph machine only costs $600. Now for the purposes of NASA and that particular flight they wanted a machine with characteristics functioning under this flight with the shock effects and the need for light weight and reliability and small size, so it cost $6,000. Now there is nothing in the nature of electrocardiographs that determines that machine. That machine was man-made according to a set of specifications. And to imply that this particular equipment somehow comes in some automatic way out of a larger body of events called the machine is simply to render this into a form of mysticism that is beyond comprehension and as a matter of fact it has the very important social effect of making people hopeless with respect not to the machine, but with respect to those who are in fact the designers and decision makers over present technology. It detracts attention from the decision makers to physical objects, and causes people to regard them as a species of idol, things having autonomous animate character. Well if men are going to worship idols, they are not going to do very well in deciding their own fate.

AUDIENCE: I'd like to direct this to Dr. Baltzell and to a lesser degree to Dr. Tumin. Both of you claimed it was necessary to have an elite. I don't believe that myself. I think that you have denied some of the implications of the new information systems which we have; what elites basically are are people with more information than other people. That is how they know what is better for other people than the people themselves. But often a person with enough information can make the best choices for himself. And so we have today, with television and radio and all the different electronic media of instantaneous information, a system by which we can give people the information by which to know what is better for themselves than anybody else. And that makes the role of an elite obsolete in a sense. The role of the elite made sense in the old mechanical society where people had to get their information from other people.

BALTZELL: I think one of the most frightening things about television is that we do not get the truth at all and it is not, as Mr. Agnew would have it, the fault of CBS or NBC. The trouble is that the dissemination of all information has to be highly selective. A couple of weeks ago, just by chance, I had the television on about four times in the day, and exactly the same scene in which the same American GI was interviewed was on all day long. They have to set this up as if it's a typical example of what's going on out there. It is very difficult.

I think competition within the elite (such as between the government and the media) is vital. As Dean Acheson said, there is no use talking to the Russians about a free press and so forth. The answer of the Russians is how much our press is surely a monopolist capitalist press. They said how much better is a wise parent who forces his children to speak the truth by punishing them when they tell falsehoods; even better is the Soviet government which makes the truth so abundantly available to all citizens there is no need for private versions and perversions of it. We know that if our government is interested in a different truth than CBS or NBC, they still must contend with the people, the elite, at the networks. The point is that, of course, we have a much more democratic society. But let me add this. A number of years ago Rockefeller said, "I'm going to wait until I get the results of the polls before I decide to run or not." *Time* magazine, whose values I do not always agree with, said the next week that he himself should have decided whether for the good of his country he should run or not and not look at the polls. Deciding on the basis of poll results brings us closer to a kind of town meeting democracy, but there is a great deal of difference between what people tell pollsters and what they think. And any pollster is biased at any rate. If I stand at 69th Street I'm going to talk to different people coming into the subway than if Mr. Tumin does. Inadvertently we will pick out different people.

TUMIN: I want to respond to the spirit of your question. You are putting together three questions: Do we need specialists to produce kinds of specialized services because they may have special talents? Secondly, do they need special conditions of work compared to others? And third, should they enjoy life more because they are specialized? Which is the elite question? The first two questions you ask are very different from the third one. We can say yes to both of the first two questions without constituting a political and a class elite. And I think that's what Dr. Baltzell would be talking about in terms of norm setting. That there are ways of arriving at common norms other than by having the elite do it. But obviously if you want to have information disseminated rapidly somebody has to find it. And there are some people better at finding information than others. And you need specialized conditions of working to find the information. So to the first two questions, yes, we need specialists and special conditions of work for them. But whether they need to enjoy a better life than others depends on the prevailing motive systems for recruiting elites. It may be that in a given market society you can't get elite specialists to take positions of specialist activities, although I doubt that, but it may not be that you can't, unless you also make them a privileged elite with regard to the enjoyment of life. But Lenin's vision was that we have a lot of technicians and a lot of people have capacities. And there is enough for everybody to go around. You don't have to pay the managers any more than you have to pay the workers.

AUDIENCE: Could you comment on the early part of Galbraith's *The New Industrial State*, where he talks about the imperatives of technology, where he contrasts Henry Ford's building his first car out of hardware store parts with the long lead time required for planning and building the first Mustang. Galbraith seems to be saying you can choose whether or not to employ modern technology, but if you do choose to exploit it, this sets certain constraints, certain imperatives for the resulting forms of social organization. There is a difference between the choice we make about what technology to use and the things we then have to do after we have chosen the technology.

MELMAN: First of all, it's undeniable that things interact. And if you extend that, you must affirm that everything affects everything else. And having done that, you are lost because the problem of science is not to affirm that things affect each other but to affirm what are the important sources of affect. It has been always understood that there will always be unexplained variance, even when you identify important causal factors. Now in the present case, it is not that wanting to make use of technology produces a certain result, it is a particular kind of decision process, overproduction, that yields the choice, the selective preference, for the present kind of design of motor vehicles and ways of making them. I will give you an example. There is endless non-standardization in our motor vehicles. The sizes of wheels, of tires, the sizes of many elemental things like ball and roller bearing, the fan belt. Visualize looking into a service station at the forest of fan belts on a wall. Now that does not result from technology. That results from social choice, economic choice. It is possible to design motor vehicles, for example, with much more standardization of components. They would not be identical vehicles, but the components could be standardized. The result would be a dramatic simplification in the sizes of factories, in the lead times required for production, and the like. So it is not technology that autonomously, in some undefined way, determines the character of the automobile organizations and the way they operate. They operate to fit the specific social criteria. Thus, it is the competitive pressure of one management in the industry to fight for a bigger proportion of the sale of automobiles that leads that particular management to try to differentiate its car from the others in some ways that are really functional and in some ways that are really just differences of floss and appearance. This is what leads management to non-standardize. Non-standardizing means that if only I put this object in my vehicle then I am the only place in the world afterwards where you can come for additional copies of this for replacement. So I guarantee myself a replacement market and a maintenance market. Well, those are not considerations of technology; those are considerations that come out of business pressure, and considerations of business advantage. So I can't go along with the notion that it's technology that determines the sizes of organizations in the broad sense that Galbraith puts it.

AUDIENCE: Are you then saying that there are no technological imperatives or just that there are fewer than Galbraith implies?

MELMAN: I am not saying that there are no consequences from particular technology. I am saying that there are no technology imperatives. There is no unified body of things that wields any imperative for anything on anybody. The size of vehicles, their horsepower, their braking capabilities, their durability, the number of parts in them, the complexity, the non-complexity has nothing to do with any technological imperative whatsoever. It is entirely a matter of choice by those who do the deciding. The lesson is this: if you want to know why technology is the way it is, find out who decides technology. That's the heart of the matter. Who decides on a particular technology? And then you can explain how it takes a particular form and has a particular characteristic. There's nothing in the design of a microphone that calls for it to have the particular sensitivities, range of response, or the durability that the microphone in front of me has. It is entirely determined by the management, which decided to build a microphone and market it for a particular purpose. If its purpose is to pick up quartets, it would be a different microphone than a microphone designed to pick up speech in an auditorium like this. If you want a microphone that will pick up voice at a distance of two feet from the speaker, it will be an entirely different microphone from the one that will pick up voice from the back of the room with the speaker standing here. In other words there is no technological imperative, there is only choice by those who decide technology.

AUDIENCE: Dr. Baltzell, when you tried looking at the conditions for which democracy would work a little bit better, you mentioned need for a better leadership. You also mentioned that the people who presently have power do not really provide the proper leadership and authority when deciding new policies. My question is, how are we going to get from this position of where people in power do not exercise the acts of leadership and authority to where we would get decent people in power with the leadership and the authority? How are they going to get the power away from those who now have it?

BALTZELL: Well, I tend to think that this is a mystery in some ways. I think that authority is far more difficult to understand than power. I think it is no accident that Mills' book was called *The Power Elite*. Because in a sense authority comes without us knowing about it. Here is a very good example of authority, to answer you in specific terms. I happened to be living in Spain the winter that de Gaulle came into France. And all of my friends there said, "Well here is the beginning of a totalitarian France." But without using terror in the manner of Hitler or Stalin, de Gaulle, for some charismatic reasons, was able to exert authority. And notice, I think, that the French would never have been able to get out of Algeria without the authority of de Gaulle. I happen to think that we cannot make up our minds about Vietnam partly because we've got a lot of people in power who do not have authority. I happen to think that these are things that arrive; I think I know a great deal about it, but it would take too much time to talk about it. But I still think that there's an element of mystery in what authority is. I have a marvelous quote from Acheson's memoirs talking about General Marshall. He said, "Nobody ever called him by his first name but his wife. As he walked into the room everybody felt his authority. He was not a martinet or a showman military man such as Patton." Then he quoted Harry Truman. Truman said, "One of the reasons why he had this was he never thought of himself." And Acheson goes on to say that the self is the ultimate corrupter. And doing your own thing is the ultimate corrupter I think; that and the obsession with self. Acheson goes on to say "And this man who was not concerned with self, had the power of ten men" or the authority of ten men. You see it is very difficult. Authority does not come from the bottom up. I think it comes from the top down. In other words, children can have power over their parents, but they do not ever have authority over their parents.

TUMIN: Could I respond to that for just a second. You know the answer to the question, how can we get leaders to act differently. One of the answers well may be, we won't. Because it all depends on how many of you there are against how many there are against you. It all depends on whether you are willing to follow the rules of democratic process or not; and if you're not, and you want to take to the streets or some other version of non-democratic process (because there are several ways of taking to the streets), then it all depends on whether the others dislike you sufficiently to shoot you down. So the answer may be that if you're not a majority, or a minority who can persuade the majority, you may never persuade the people up there to do what you want instead of what they want. And then it may be your fate to be in a perpetual minority. Which by the way, depending on how repressive the majority is, is not such a bad condition to be in. If you assume that the majority represents the least common denominator of wisdom, then it's not a bad condition at all.

AUDIENCE: I would like to ask the panel and the people here in general what we are doing determining what the world needs. Have you ever talked with people and asked them? As the son of a blue collar worker, I find it frightening when we ask "which elite are we going to substitute for which."

TUMIN: I think I understand your question. If you mean are we going to get into the concerns that are felt by a variety of common men then I think that the answer is absolutely yes. And at the only level to which we are appropriate, which is the consideration of the interlocking of ideas presumably based upon a great deal of knowledge about the previous experiences of men on a highly analytical level which can provide certain general propositions that serve as guidelines for thinking; guidelines which then may be useful in a whole host of applied problems at community organization levels, at factory organization levels, union organization levels, management-union relationships. It is only at that level that we are appropriate. It would be wrong to ask us to be appropriate at the level of what should be the next tactic for this particular union or group of community people to do with regard to the problems of their neighborhood. We would be presumptuous to consider ourselves appropriate to that level. So if you are asking, "Are we relevant?" Absolutely. In the only way we can be. Are we immediately relevant? Absoutely not. I do not know any other way to answer you.

MELMAN: Now, I am a professor in an engineering school. Engineers for about a quarter century have been pre-eminently concerned with servicing the requirements of the central state, mainly its military arms. Especially in the last fifteen years, the training of technologists has proceeded with major emphasis in generating men and women trained in knowledge that is serviceable to the kinds of designs, to the kinds of technologies and artifacts that the military and space organizations want. If you would like to see some major alteration in the nature of the technology produced, get to know the engineers and try to persuade them about the new values that they ought to incorporate in their work. This society now suffers from the burden of having a great many able men who have been trained to do design service, technology service, for military space organizations rather than in the service of all men or of civilian technology. I feel a certain kind of despair from the flood of queries about the effects of technology, that autonomous entity, while people everywhere in the university system fail to go to the part of the university which is in fact the source of technology and the training of technologists and try to cope there in a *political* way, because that is what the problem is: persuading people to revise their values in terms of the needs of society, in terms of your values, and in terms of the technologies and kindred effects from them that might be deemed desirable. The discussion in the absence of such effort takes on a certain quality of unreality because if you talk about these matters in an analytically abstracted manner entirely, a social science standpoint, then you are left in a position of powerlessness. The only way to exercise power, if you please, to influence decision making in these matters is to work with the technologists on the curricula and the whole process that produces the character of technology and society.

AUDIENCE: It seems to me, Dr. Melman, you put great emphasis on decision makers plus the technologist. But it seems to me that the market has a much greater influence on things. If you are going to understand the design of a machine you have to go back to the social forces, the families, the towns which influence the market.

MELMAN: Well, let's understand the matter flat out. The market of the last two decades has been the Department of Defense. And those producing for it—that's the market. And engineering curricula and the functioning of society and the performance of engineers have been heavily oriented to that direction. That is why we have electrocardiograph machines costing $6,000 instead of more serviceable ones. That is why the military electronics in the United States is heavily developed, but it was left to the electronics industry of Japan to make high class, low cost, reasonably efficient consumer electronics. The engineers have to fight to serve in the market. You do not have to bring in the family in order to cope with that. The engineers have been trained to serve the Department of Defense and NASA and the companies who are under contract to them.

AUDIENCE: It just seems to me that you have to look at where the decisions for the Department of Defense are coming from. You have to look to Congress, to the whole culture that demands this type of defense machinery and not just to . . .

MELMAN: Well, first of all, the entire country lends itself to being persuaded to support the ideology of the cold war, and was in support of the political parties and the political leaders who dramatized and gave voice to it. The country is getting the Congress that it elected; don't ever forget that. They really do elect them.

TUMIN: If you are asking us to take more effective means to account for the nature of consumer demands as they may shape the design of technology, especially consumer technology, aside from industrial technology on the larger scale, I think it's a perfectly reasonable question to ask to what extent that has come to be a major influence on engineering thinking and design. It is a very complex decision-making process which does involve some advertising, which does involve some consumer research. It involves some preposterous notions about the psychology of consumer demand. For example, whiskey manufacturers are told to create a whiskey that will have the appearance of unpainted beams to give us the feeling of the natural cask which will bring man closer to nature, because man feels alienated from nature. Believe me that is the language which they talk. And there are distinctions for the ladies between various kinds of Breck shampoo that were designed presumably on the basis of the extent of your ego security system. I think the most evident manifestation of the appearance of consumer demand as a significant fact in the shaping of design is the version of it epitomized in Ralph Nader's work. I think that is the stage we're at now with regard to how consumer demand works to shape design; that we are now an increasingly vocal and increasingly listened to source of complaint. I think it will be a long time before a genuine concern for the artistry and the comfort of living by consumers in the family and in the home will be seriously taken into account in any way other than such items as the particular shape of the doors on a two-door refrigerator, in terms of how much freezer and how much non-freezer space people want, and whether women are left-handed or right-handed, and whether they like the refrigerator by the sink or not. But I think that it's only beginning to emerge that the consumer is making something of a difference other than those large-scale consumers called the army and defense establishments who can give specifications as to how many people they want to kill at what cost.

4

Symposium on Technology and the Counterculture

Edgar Z. Friedenberg

I am going to try to put out one set of relationships that has been troubling me with regard to how technology affects the position of the counterculture and let other people respond to it so that we can argue about it. I think it probably will arouse a certain amount of argument because it relates what seems to me to be an important built-in conflict that I think is seldom acknowledged. I myself am very much encouraged by the emergence of the values represented in the counterculture. I am using the term as Theodore Roszak uses it, as Phillip Slater uses it—you might think of it as the hippie-organic food-communal kind of thing; not that any one of these is necessarily the life style you adopt, but that particular conception of where to look for freedom, value, and meaning in life as it relates to as much of it as you can dig at any one time. This is the kind of thing that has meant increasingly a lot to me in the past few years.

This means then that where I have to make political decisions the enhancement of the chance of the counterculture, its support, if necessary its defense, trying to keep it from being busted, trying to find a place to practice it where it won't be busted, weigh very heavily in my decisions. When the counterculture first began to emerge, that is when kids began moving out to communes; or where the kinds of music, the kinds of celebrations that express what they say is meaning in their lives were first practiced, I don't think we were clear as to what the political relationships of that to the other forces in the United States were. I think these relationships have become clearer now.

I have reached the conclusion that the kinds of values that underlie what I enjoy most in life really are elitist. This is true in the current American context, and as far back as I can see in American history, this always would have been elitist, and I'm going to suggest that I personally am more than willing to settle for that. I think when the Monterey Pop Festival first emerged most of my friends would have thought that this was a pattern that in its freedom, at least in its expression of feelings and the use it would make of resources, could have been adopted as an alternative for a great many people. Consequently we found ourselves in a political bag that included a great many who since became recognizable as our mortal enemies and who should perhaps not be blamed for that because they never asked us to include them with us in the first place.

I think this can be seen with regard to some of the specific issues and what happens when you actually begin to pursue them. Take for example the environmental thing, the controversy over whether to preserve the natural state of rivers or to build dams and make water available for power and recreational lakes and so on. It is really quite clear that there are people who would prefer, as I do, that the environment be preserved, indeed urge the utilization of nature in ways that will prevent national parks from being of the greatest popular value or set up to provide a wide range of values to more people. It is perfectly true, as the Federal Reclamation Service argues, that more people are going to come water skiing on that artifical lake than would ever manage to get down to the unspoiled canyon, and I'm still for the unspoiled canyon and I want to be clear that I'm being honest about that. I have no fantasy in my mind that somehow the masses of Salt Lake City, when there get to be masses in Salt Lake City, would have found their way down into southern Utah had the canyon been left there for them. The problem becomes more obvious if you look at things like the kind of controversy that went on in southern South Carolina about whether the beach should be held unspoiled or a chemical company should be allowed to move in and build a factory that would have employed a great many people. It's perfectly clear that there would have been pollution. It's perfectly clear that it would have made jobs. It's perfectly clear that those jobs would have provided opportunities to South Carolina blacks who have now no alternative except rather unpleasant domestic employment. I'd rather see the seashore saved than the opportunity enhanced under those conditions. But I do not want to pose as someone who is a friend of every kind of freedom and advancement and to deny that the elitist choice is implicit in the position that I take.

The matter becomes even more clearly political when we consider the kinds of music, the kinds of literature, and so on that get busted in this country as long as there is the freedom of popular expression and litigation to make the general opinion the prevailing and legally enforceable norm. I do not think that is going to change. I don't even think that you are going to find a large proportion of the American people really turned off by the My Lai episode and the others that we know have gone along with it. And I would be prepared if necessary to turn my back on that in order to find some life space for the kinds of things that mean most to me. If there was anyone to fight I would rather fight here, but you can't tell your friends from your enemies very well in this kind of situation. The assertion of the values on the basis of which the war in Indo-China could be condemned gets all mixed up with the defense of the dominance of the majority—a majority which apparently simply is not sufficiently repelled by the war to regard Lt. Calley, for example, as a more serious threat to human life than Charles Manson (considering that the two cases reached their first stage of decision at the same time). So there essentially is where the political issue is for me at the moment.

There is one more example, another case of the same thing. Let me try to make the thing concrete with reference to the schools. I'm very much opposed to the continuation of compulsory school attendance, and in fact I guess I was the first person to specifically come out against it in *Coming of Age in America*.[1] The position has been much more fully developed by Ivan Illich at the Center for Inter-Cultural Documentation and Everett Reimer, who works there with him. Ivan Illich, in his new book *Deschooling Society*,[2] and Reimer in *School is dead: alternatives in education*,[3] advocate the replacement of compulsory school attendance, not just establishing experimental schools, or anything else relatively as small in its effect as the Christopher Jencks voucher system (though I think it is good as far as it goes), but rather the establishment of alternative networks of resources so that people who wanted to learn something could get support from the state to study the subject with other people who are interested in it when they wanted to. This would not be under circumstances that would permit the accumulation of a credential in early life that would be of much, if any, value for social and economic mobility. The emphasis rather is on getting the resources devoted to learning for people who want to learn, when they want to learn, regardless of what other good it might do them or at what disadvantage they might find themselves in competition with other people who had been more gung-ho about doing what they are conventionally supposed to do.

Well, when you make this kind of proposal, often the question is raised, "But won't that decrease equality of opportunity in any culture that adopts it? Will that not in effect remove the schools as the ladder by which people who aspire to make it within the culture can do so? Is this not going to be insulting to all of the persons who as discriminated minorities would be only too glad to meet with that Dow Chemical recruiter, if they ever got to college, or to accept a commission as an officer in the United States Army when they're the first member of their family even to get to college? Isn't this going to be hard lines on them?"

There are ways in which you can argue that maybe it would be that ultimately the quality of life would generally improve enough so that all would benefit. Perhaps, but I'm not convinced that that's so; I don't really think it's so, and the fact that it probably isn't so doesn't turn me off. I still favor letting people who don't want to go to school not go to school, even with the awareness that they would probably disproportionately be the middle class or the privileged who had certain other ways of making it toward where they wanted to go without having to take on the entire system. I do not want to delude people into thinking that what I was arguing for could be justified as in the general interest and as a promotion of the general welfare. I don't think it is; that isn't my bag.

Notes

1. Edgar Z. Friedenberg, *Coming of Age in America* (New York: Random House, 1965).

2. Ivan D. Illich, *Deschooling Society* (New York: Harper & Row, 1971).

3. Everett K. Reimer, *School is dead: alternatives in education,* Garden City: Doubleday, 1971.

Nat Hentoff

Wine lore is full of stories of wines which, however great they may have been at their places of origin, simply do not travel well. Unfortunately, this was Nat Hentoff's reaction to the transcript of his opening remarks at the Counterculture Symposium. He did not feel that there was any reasonable way that he could revise his address so that it would meet his standards for written work. He asked, therefore, that we summarize his major points so that the continuity of this transcription of the Counterculture Symposium could be preserved.

1. Hentoff said he sees technology as a neutral tool. The real issue is the social and political control of technology and its effects. When he first read Ellul's *The Technological Society* he was fascinated but not fully persuaded by Ellul's argument that technology is an autonomous force with the power to influence institutions and culture. However, he is even less persuaded by that thesis as time goes by.

2. He thinks "counterculture" is a hard term to get a hold of. Its underlying values are represented by several very different life styles: from A.J. Muste and Cesar Chavez to the hippie-communal life referred to by Edgar Friedenberg in his presentation. He questioned the durability of the latter life style and wondered whether many of its young middle class participants will just move quite easily into the institutional structure of the larger society, smoking marijuana instead of drinking cocktails. For example, Hentoff suggested that *Gimme Shelter* is an important political film because of the picture it presents of a maleable mass being told what to do, with no apparent realization of its own potential power to prevent the violence which occurred in its midst at the rock concert at Altamont.

3. Hentoff said he did not share Friedenberg's apparent concern about the public reaction to the verdict in the Calley trial, because he felt that a substantial percentage of the population did not believe that Calley was innocent or to be commended, but that he had been made a scapegoat. This means that if he were going to be tried and sentenced, so should Westmoreland, Johnson, McNamara, and the other political and military leaders responsible for the war. Hentoff also observed that while assessing public opinion polls was really Professor Lipset's department, he agreed with Allard Lowenstein that 23 million new young voters would be a significant liberal factor in 1972, regardless of what political analysts like Scammon and Wattenberg say.

4. Based on visits to a great many schools in black, Puerto Rican, and Chicano neighborhoods, Hentoff's reported impression was that, even if these minorities get equality of opportunity and education, they will not be as eager to sign up with the major corporations or with the military as some people think. There is definitely a change in consciousness and, while these people clearly want more social, economic, and political power than they now have,

they also will be more selective than his (Hentoff's) generation was about the places in society they are willing to occupy.

5. He agreed with Friedenberg that the compulsory education law should be abolished, but disagreed quite strongly with Ivan Illich's position of total deschooling. Hentoff expressed the fear that this would work to the disadvantage of the so-called "inner-city" children insofar as being able to drop out of the system and then come back in at will is a white middle class privilege. Deschooling would also work against the progress which is now being made in school decentralization and community control, which among other things is facilitating the promotion of blacks into such positions as district superintendent.

6. Returning more directly to the relationship between technology and social change, Hentoff cited a quotation from Karl Marx which bears on the question of where the control of social change lies and why he does not fully accept Ellul's position:

The materialist doctrine that men are products of circumstances and upbringing and that, therefore, changed men are products of other circumstances and changed upbringing, forgets that it is men that change circumstances. . . .[1]

Hentoff concluded his remarks with a commentary on the nature of human nature. In his view human nature exists as revolutionary potential. The consequence of this revolutionary potential is that human nature can not be judged in terms of prevailing conceptions of good and evil but it does have the power to actively change the circumstances of its existence. Hentoff said that for all of his reservations about certain aspects of the counterculture, he thinks it definitely has a sense of possibility for achieving social change. It is with this sense of possibility that discussions of technology, counterculture, and the future should begin.

Note

1. Karl Marx, "Theses on Feuerbach," in Karl Marx and Friedrich Engels, *Basic Writings on Politics and Philosophy*, edited by Lewis S. Feuer (Garden City: Anchor Books, 1959), p. 244.

Seymour Martin Lipset

Insofar as there is a disagreement between Mr. Friedenberg and Mr. Hentoff, I would like to come down on the side of Mr. Hentoff; I believe I am an egalitarian, as Mr. Hentoff is. Mr. Friedenberg is an avowed elitist. He quite openly and honestly propogates elitist values in the context of this discussion of the counterculture and technology.

But before going into some of these issues, I can't help but pick up one point that Nat Hentoff challenged me on: my use of polling statistics. I would, therefore, like to use some particularly interesting ones here. I would like to suggest that if you who are younger think you are more virtuous than we who are older, the polls demonstrate you are wrong in terms of the very issues about which the more vociferous among you are most concerned. The fact that the Vietnam war is a horror, a mistake, a blunder, whatever words one wants to call it, was recognized earlier and most continually by people over fifty than by younger age groups. Every poll taken from 1965 to the most recent one I have seen in May 1971, which reported on answers to whether the Vietnam war is a mistake or not, correlated by age, shows the younger the group, the fewer who say it is a mistake. The older group has been much more likely to say it is a mistake. Of course, the proportion in the population who say it is a mistake has steadily increased since 1965, until by now the large majority of every age group thinks entering the war was a mistake. But the percentage of those under thirty who will not admit that it was a mistake, according to Gallup Poll in May 1971, is still close to 40 percent. If recognizing that the Vietnam war was wrong is a measure of the intelligence of different generations, then the older people are a lot more intelligent than the younger.

The same conclusion may be reached if we judge the age groups by their voting preferences. In 1968, the younger people were more likely to have voted for George Wallace. We did not have the eighteen-year-old vote then, but a national high school poll taken by some people at Purdue in 1968 reported that the proportion of high school students who were for Mr. Wallace was even higher than among the twenty-one to twenty-five year olds. If you think that the youth who were for Mr. Wallace were for him because they just did not like what was being done by the machine hacks in the old party, you are wrong. Those who voted for Mr. Wallace in every age group were much more for the Vietnam war and against blacks than those who preferred Humphrey or Nixon. Wallace in recent (1971) opinion surveys continues to do best among the new eighteen-to-twenty-one-year old section of the electorate. (You can find these data and my discussion of them, together with various references to materials which I have quoted in this talk in my recently published Little, Brown paperback book, *Rebellion in the University*).[1]

It is unfortunate, but true, that there is no special set of political virtues attached to being young. As Aristotle noted 2500 years ago, youth are more passionate, more sure of themselves, more idealistic, more willing to risk all. But such qualities may be enlisted for a variety of causes, pacifism and war, leftist radicialism today, but fascism yesterday. (The Nazis won their first majorities among any group in Germany in student council elections in various universities in 1931, while they were still relatively weak among other strata. The Italian Fascists also glorified youth. Their party song was "Giovinezza" ("Youth") and they, too, had a great deal of student backing before Mussolini took power. During the 1930s, fascist parties from Spain to Finland found that they did better within the universities than elsewhere.)

To get back to the Friedenberg-Hentoff conflict, as Hentoff suggested, for some decades now government has been the only agency involved in extending benefits to the less privileged at the expense of the elite. To get back to technology, the current question is not whether we can restrain technology, or some of the dysfunctional effects of technology, pollution, and the like in America. The main issue, as Hentoff suggested, is one of power, of social and economic class relationships on a worldwide scale. We live in a world in which most people outside of America and northern Europe are poor, miserably poor; that is most of the three billion people now in the world, or the six billion who will be in the world by the year 2000. The rich, including the rich American college students, cannot demand a clean world for themselves, at the expense of the poor. This is true even within the United States. The demand to limit the use of beaches to a small population is a proposal to enhance the income and life style of the rich. This may be illustrated from a Massachusetts example. A few years ago, most of Cape Cod was declared a national park. This meant and means that nobody can build in the Cape Cod National Park area, except the people who then owned property in that area. They have seen the value of their property double and triple, in just a few years. It will continue to skyrocket as the years go by. To my mind this approach to protecting the beaches and the ponds of Cape Cod is an example of the rich keeping their environment clean and making money while doing it.

The same point may be made about other countries. There has probably been a greater increase in pollution in Tokyo than in any other great city in the world. The only realistic alternative to the rapid rate of economic growth and corresponding increase in the standard of living of the people of Japan over the last twenty-five years, which has polluted Tokyo and other parts of the country, would have meant that the mass of the Japanese would live in stinking hovels. The same choice was made in Russia. The Soviets have largely ignored problems of pollution; they have invested all they could in industrial growth.

I'm not in favor of what the Japanese or the Soviets have done with respect to pollution, but planners and government officials must deal with real alternatives, and I'm not sure they were wrong to have gone hell bent for more production in both countries. If the alternatives are a low standard of living for the masses or more dirt in the air, and the former means more deaths, high infant mortality and the like, I don't think offhand that I would condemn the people who decided for technological development even though it meant more dirt. We should fight to clean up the dirt, but advocating cleanliness, just saying let's be Mr. Clean, is not a moral proposal, particularly if you're rich, as all of us in this room are, as compared to most people.

It is vital that we deal with the basic issue, fantastic population growth, realistically. The real "solution" to the cleanliness problem, if there is a "solution" to problems of pollution, for a country like America, is probably negative population growth, that is, a declining population. To do this, however, would raise other issues, which I can't go into here in detail. What, for example, would the meaning of family be, in a world in which most people do not have children?

To turn briefly to the general issue of counterculture, which is an aspect of what brings us together, we can not have a discussion about this unless we reach some clarification about the term *counterculture*. It has been used in ways which make it meaningless. For example, though I admired A.J. Muste, and I support the work being done in California to organize farm workers by Cesar Chavez and others, I do not consider A.J. Muste or Cesar Chavez as being representative of or involved in the counterculture, unless by the word counterculture you mean anybody who is outside the mainstream. By that criterion, of course, both of them are very much part of a counterculture. But the counterculture concept to which I think we are addressing ourselves today involves a rejection of the dominant cultural ethos of the larger society in terms of personal style and way of life. When those who use the term refer to the counterculture, they are usually referring to a kind of hedonistic expressive style with respect to dress, hairstyles, and beards, use of drugs, new and freer sex relationships, non-careerist behavior with respect to jobs, and so forth.

It is important to note that such behavior is not, in my judgment, the outgrowth of a reaction to present day technology, as Reich has suggested. It can better be understood as conformity to a social "law," of limited possibilities. To put it in other words, every yes has a no; every plus has a minus; everything that is, has an opposite. If you reject what is, you often have a limited set of alternatives. If you read through the literature on youth and student protest historically and comparatively, the extent to which the dominant behavior patterns repeat, ever since 1800 in the United States and Europe is fantastic.

The first such movement in nineteenth century Europe were the Borschen-schatten, organizations of German students circa 1815, who in protest to life in Germany developed a "counterculture." It took the form of special moustaches, beards, long hair, colorful clothes, unwashed skin, rough clothing. The description of their clothes suggest they looked very much like the hippies of today. They also defended their counterculture in populist terms, i.e., styles of the common people.

Going on in time, one finds again and again illustrations of the same law of limited possibilities, or perhaps limited imagination. The California sociologist Cesar Graña, in a book on the emergence of the Paris bohemia,[2] described life among students in the 1830s and 1840s in the same area, St. Germain du Pris, where the May 1968 "events" took place, in terms which sound like Telegraph Ave. in the late 1960s.

[They] held radical-sounding, erratic political ideas which somehow were never followed by practical action. According to Balzac they could be recognized by their off-center cravats, greasy coats, long beards, and dirty fingernails. The Bohemians of the 1830's and 40's were young, actually and ideologically; they claimed youth itself was the collective expression of genius. . . . In all accounts of the Bohemia of the Orleanist years [the 1840's], the first impressions have always to do with its ingenious techniques of social outrage. When Thackeray first came on the Paris Bohemia, he was astonished enough to make a careful record of their appearance—their ringlets, straight locks, toupees, English, Greek and Spanish hair nets, and the variety of their beards and jackets.

The Russian students of the 1870s and 1880s also "invented" a counter-culture. The *Encyclopedia Britannica* (1911 edition) describes them as follows:

Among the students of the universities and higher technical schools [there appeared] . . . a new and striking original type—young men and women in slovenly attire, who called in question and ridiculed the generally received convictions and respectable conventions of social life. . . . They reversed the traditional order of things even to the trivial matters of external appearance, the males allowing the hair to grow long and the females cutting it short, and adding sometimes the additional badge of blue spectacles. Their appearance, manners and conversation were apt to shock ordinary people, but to this they were profoundly indifferent, for they had raised themselves above the level of so-called public opinion, despised Phillistine respectability, and rather liked to scandalize people still under the influence of what they considered antiquated prejudices.

I should note here, parenthetically, that when Bakunin, the famous Russian anarchist, reported that, because of persecution, thousands of Russian students were going to emigrate to Western Europe and join the radical movement there, Friedrich Engels wrote a letter to Karl Marx in which he noted his dismay that there were thousands of revolutionary students in Russia. "If there is anything that might ruin the Western Europe Socialist movement it would be this import of 40,000 more or less educated ambitious hungry Russian nihilists." That judgment of the counterculture by Engels was to be repeated time and again down to 1970 by various Marxists. In 1920, Lenin complained about the sexual and drinking habits of the radical youth in the West. He said: "The revolution . . . can not tolerate orgiastic conditions. . . . Dissoluteness . . . is bourgeois, is a phenomenon of decay. . . . I am deeply concerned about the future of our youth." Clearly what bothered him then was behavior comparable to that of recent years among alienated youth in America.

The law of limited possibilities may be illustrated with respect to the American past as well. The 1920s, for example, though not characterized by extensive campus political protest, was a period of counterculture behavior with respect to sex, dress styles, and law and order. And on an ideological level, one found an emphasis on antagonism to technology. A large student movement arose which centered around a magazine called *The New Student*. In a statement in 1923, almost fifty years ago, *The New Student* expressed the ideology of this movement of the 1920s in the following terms:

We do not believe it is any longer possible for the American college to give an education to its students. . . . Spiritually this is an age of ruin—of nausea. We suspect that many of our elders retain the 19th century belief in science and knowledge. We cannot share it. We need a faith. . . . At least we know what must go.

Mechanization must go. A certain scholarly, scientific attitude must go. The values for which we are searching do not seem susceptible of proof, of capture by the "scientific spirit." The faith, the assumptions on which science rests are lacking, hence there are no "social sciences." Moreover we need to look ahead; and creative thought is different in kind from mere knowledge. . . .

We cannot even accept the leadership of the younger [faculty]. . . . The forces of decay are so strong that we cannot trust a cocksure psychology or "radical" sociology.

This was published in 1923!

These similarities in style of protest, in the orientation of youth and student movements in a variety of countries over two centuries, do not mean an identical pattern of causation or of functional significance for participants. What differentiates most of them has often been much greater than what is comparable. But noting the recurring similarities in youth and student "counterculture" should innoculate us to avoid jumping to the conclusion that the most recent expression of such behavior is the inevitable outcome of an endemic structural trend, of factors inherent in technological or other structural changes. An examination of past efforts to explain periods of youth unrest indicates considerable similarities in the causal interpretations over a sixty year stretch in America. Repeatedly intellectuals have interpreted such developments as reactions to rapid technological changes, particularly in the media, and of a resultant breakdown of religion and family discipline. Again, to give an early example of this, *The Atlantic Monthly*, in 1911, before World War I, had a debate about the source of the youth rebelliousness, of the "culte de moi," current among the affluent student youth of that day. One writer, Cornelia Comer, described this as a response to the fact that in 1911 young people did not read books any more; nor did they study hard as her generation had done. Rather, she argued, the present generation had its tastes formed by frequent attendance at "the continuous vaudeville and the motion picture shows." Parents, she stated, were too afraid to keep their children at home when "all the other children are allowed to go to the movies." Parents supposedly did not teach the moral beliefs that the previous generation had learned when young, because these now appeared to be old fashioned. Two months after that article, Randolph Borne, a brilliant young socialist, then an undergraduate activist at Columbia, replied by agreeing with Cornelia Comer that rapid technological change and weak home discipline had affected the views of youth. He concluded, however, that those of his generation could see more clearly precisely because they were freer than previous generations from allegiance to outmoded beliefs and that, therefore, they were actually better educated than their parents had been. He credited this freedom to their exposure to the new forms of mass media which had broadened their views. Those born in "an age of newspapers, free libraries and cheap magazines . . . [can] necessarily get a broader horizon than the preceding generation had. We see what is going on in the world, and we get a clash of different points of view, to an extent which was impossible to our fathers."

The explanations of the counterculture of the 1920s, of the "generation gap," between those under and over thirty years of age (so help me this was what they wrote and talked about also), again pointed to the impact of technological change. Writers of the 1920s stressed the effects of the automobile and radio in weakening home teaching and in exposing the young to a diversity of ideas and experiences. The census of 1920 had recorded an urban majority for the first time in American history. And John Gavit, a journalist, in a book dealing with the behavior of college students, argued that urbanization meant a sharp reduction in the time spent by parents with children, a reduction in "the sense of responsibility—to neighborhood public opinion and standards," and more time spent by parents in pleasure seeking activities, the result of this was permissiveness in child rearing, or plain neglect. Like earlier analysts, he suggested that young people "whose home experience has given them no standards, or no self control with which to enforce such as they have, always go to pieces, when superimposed restraints are lifted."

Other analysts of that day put the responsibility for campus unrest, for the uneasiness of the students, on the universities themselves, on what was going on in them. They criticized the faculty for their careerist research orientation. Such comments, in fact, go back to the late nineteenth century. Repeatedly, every time students protested, books and articles appeared attacking the lack of concern for students, bad teaching, impersonal relationships, and so forth. There is a story, which some of you may have heard, told about the university today, which goes something like this. A man reports he had been talking to the dean of a university and had asked him who's the best teacher on the faculty. The dean replied, "Assistant Professor A. He is very good. He is a brilliant lecturer, his students like him, he spends time with them, and so on." The story teller said: I suppose he will be getting tenure. The Dean answered, "Well no, he hasn't done anything." A version of this tale was published by Abraham Flexner in 1909 in the *Atlantic Monthly*. You can find a lot more material dealing with the recurrent discussions of faculty-student relationships in my book, so I will drop the subject here.

Not only have the technological interpretations of youth unrest been similar, but the adult criticisms, even, or especially from leading radical leftists been comparable. Essentially they have been bothered by the politically counter-productive consequences of youth engaging in what we now call, in jargon, expressive behavior. That is, doing their thing. I mentioned earlier that Friedrich Engels and Karl Marx had frowned on such behavior in the nineteenth century. Lenin denounced it as counter productive in the 1920s. More recently, Madam Nguyen Thi Binh, the N.L.F. (Viet Cong) foreign minister, told visitors from the United States that American student protestors are responsible for helping to prolong the Vietnam war, because rather than concentrating on what she felt was the important thing, namely the resistance to the war, they antagonize older people, who are as anti-war as they are, by their exotic life styles and expressive forms of personal behavior. She said the Vietnamese people and American soldiers are paying for the elitist tendencies of American students. Eldridge Cleaver also expressed a similar point of view, thus shifting some of his own opinions. He criticized the counterculture as harmful to the political cause, and argued that using drugs is a form of escape from involvement in politics, of confrontation with the system.

I will end this with one further point. There is a great deal of academic research on the topic of student unrest. Many find it useful to differentiate between alienated students who are involved in various forms of political action and protest, and those who are primarily engaged in expressive counterculture activity. The investigators report interesting and sharp differences between them. The political protestors tend to come from families whose political and social outlook is similar, though of course usually not as radical, as their own. That is, the parents of left wing student protestors tend to be liberal to left in their politics. Thus, though they may think their children are going too far, are too violent or aggressive, nevertheless, they're on the same side of the political spectrum as their activist offspring. The counterculture people, those who are described as hippies, bohemians, beatnicks, and so forth, tend to come from conservative family backgrounds. They are the ones who are in a generation conflict with their parents. They exhibit various indications of being in a state of severe tension, both before and since they've adopted the expressive personal style of the counterculture. The research data suggest that the others, those for whom politics is a more instrumental form of activity, who find reinforcement for their political alienation in their family background, are much less involved in counterculture activity, particularly with respect to use of drugs, than those who are involved in fighting their parents. While it may be very nice to have wealthy kids fight their parents, this is not the way revolutions are made, Charles Reich and others to the contrary.

Notes

1. Seymour Martin Lipset, *Rebellion in the University* (Boston: Little Brown, 1971).

2. Cesar Graña, *Modernity and Its Discontents* (New York: Harper Torchbooks, 1964).

Ira Einhorn

Ira Einhorn attended the University of Pennsylvania and still lives near the campus. He is well known locally as a member of the counterculture and frequent interpreter of it to the straight culture. To demonstrate some of the potential freedom of modern technology, he and several of his friends brought an assortment of public address and closed circuit television equipment to the Counterculture Symposium. In his opening presentation he used this equipment and also moved around to various parts of the auditorium. As a result, the tape recording of his remarks was less than complete. Even if it had been complete, the transcribed text really would not have captured the feeling Einhorn was trying to create. Instead, he has asked that we print what follows. Within the limits of the print medium it does a better job of capturing both the substance and the spirit of his symposium presentation than would even a revised transcript of the verbal portion of his performance.

THE EVOLUTION OF THE SORCERERS' APPRENTICE
(FOR ED BACON)
HUBRIS
"CRUDE AND IMPERFECT, MAGIC IS STILL MAN'S FIRST
CONSCIOUS ABSTRACTION FROM NATURE, HIS FIRST ATTEMPT
TO LINK DISPARATE OBJECTS BY SOME UNSEEN ATTRACTION
BETWEEN THEM."
LOREN EISELEY
SCIENCE IS THE MAGIC OF THIS SEASON'S DESIRE
THE WEATHER OF THE TIME'S MIND
APPLIED
LIKE A TOURNIQUET
TO THE BLOOD OF OUR NATURAL OBSERVATION
FLAYING SQUAMOUS NATURE
WITH A RATIONAL WHIP
WHOSE CORDS
THREATEN
THE VERY EXISTENCE
OF THE BLOOD
DENYING
IN ITS EXUBERANT OVERREACHING
THE VERY SPIRIT THAT SUSTAINS

"BREAKDOWN
U
T
IS

BREAKTHROUGH

LIGHT
COMING IN
NEW
FORMS

$E = MC^2$ EXPLODING

NEW HORIZONS
NEW EXTENSIONS
A SOCIETY BUILT
ON
TECHNOLOGY
A HOUSE BUILT
BY   I.B.M.

COMMUNICATIONS
                    THROUGH THE COURTESY OF
Ma BELL
            EXTENSIONS
            TECHNOLOGY
A MEANS
            FOR DEALING WITH e^x INCREASING
ENERGY

            CANCER IS A NEGATIVE MEANS
                        OF
DEALING WITH INCREASING SOMATIC
                    ENERGY
INTERNALIZED
        &
            USED INCORRECTLY

            THE QUEST FOR IMMORTALITY
                    IS IN ITSELF
THE FEAR OF DEATH

            MATTER IS A TEMPORARY STATE
OF MATERIAL

CRYSTALLIZATION

    IN
            THE VAST DIRAC OCEAN
OF
    COSMIC MATTER

    THE ATTEMPT
                    TO MAKE A FORM PERMANENT
IS ANTIFLOW
            ANTIEVOLUTIONARY
THE STRIVING
            FOR IMMORTALITY OF THE
    CANCER CELL
                    IS
                    NEGATIVE FEEDBACK
    AN INDICATOR
            THAT WE NEED NEW LIMBS

NEW EXTENSIONS
NEW MODES
OF GOING ON

SOMA

IS

AT

TERMINUS—ALL FURTHER
EVOLUTION IS IN REALM OF CONSCIOUSNESS
CONSCIOUSNESS

WILL CONTINUE TO EXTEND
ITSELF

WITH OR WITHOUT

NATURE   THE BODY

THE NATURAL, THE NORM
IS OLD FORM

18th CENTURY TOTALIZATION
NOW

SURROUNDED BY

3 ENVIRONMENTS
2 VISIBLE

a. MECHANICAL
b. ELECTRICAL
1 INVISIBLE

c. MAGNETIC

TECHNOLOGY HAS PREVIOUSLY BEEN AN
EXTENSION

OF   **BODYFORMS**
NOW

THE EXTENSIONS
ARE OF THE NERVOUS SYSTEM
THE BRAIN
& FINALLY

CONSCIOUSNESS ITSELF
SOON

THE HUMAN MODULE
WILL ITSELF

BE TOTALLY EXTERIORIZED

AS

THE TRIP TO THE MOON
SYMBOLIZES

                    THE POSSIBILITY OF TOTALLY
EXTERIORIZING
                    OUR SURROUND
                        UNWELT
                        ENVIRONMENT
                        ECOLOGY

POLLUTION
                    IS THE FRICTION OF INTERFACE
UNCATEGORIZED
                    ENERGY THAT IS LOST IN
THE CONVERSION
        TRANSFORMATION
                            FROM
THE OLD MECHANICAL
                        TO THE NEW ELECTRICAL
                    ENVIRONMENT
JUST AS STRESS
            INFORMATION OVERLOAD
IS THE BYPRODUCT
                OF THE TRANSITION FROM
AN OLD MECHANICAL
TO A NEW ELECTRICAL
                    CONSCIOUSNESS

BOTH POLLUTION AND STRESS
                            ARE FALLOUT
STRESS IS THE PHOTONS
            OF
        CONSCIOUSNESS
AS IT IS QUANTIZED
    IN ITS
            TRANSITION
FROM
        ONE LEVEL
                    OF CONSCIOUSNESS
        TO
                            ANOTHER
        THE NEGATIVE
                        INTERPRETATION
OF BOTH STRESS AND POLLUTION
IS A CONCEPTUAL FAILURE
AN INABILITY

TO DEAL WITH THE NEW IN A POSITIVE FASHION
IT IS A REGRESSIVE MODE
OF
DEALING WITH THE

UNEXPECTED

THE NEW

JACQUES ELLUL AND THOSE WHO SHARE HIS HELL
ASCRIBE
A DAEMONIC SEPARATE LIFE TO TECHNOLOGY
THAT IT DOES NOT POSSESS

TECHNOLOGY ≡ TOOL

NOT

TOY

IF MEN PLAY WITH GREAT FORCES THEY
DO
NOT
UNDERSTAND
THEY
WILL
PRODUCE
GREAT DE-STRUCTION

$$E = MC^2$$

EINSTEIN—1905
DOES NOT
INEVITABLY LEAD
TO

HIROSHIMA

AMERIKA—1945
THIS TRANSITION
IS NOT INHERENT
IN NUCLEAR TECHNOLOGY

THE LAW OF CAUSE & EFFECT
DOES NOT CONTAIN THOSE
WHO
CAN OVERVIEW IT
IT BECOMES
TOOL RATHER THAN SURROUND

A TOOL THAT CAN BE USED
IN A POSITIVE CONSCIOUS WAY
     TECHNOLOGY NEED NOT CONTROL MAN
     MAN CAN CONTROL IT
        ONCE
HE   LEARNS   TO   CONTROL   HIMSELF
      UNTIL
         SELF CONTROL IS LEARNED
EXTENSIONS
      WILL BE OUT OF CONTROL

PLANETARY METABOLISM

     IS PRESENTLY
        HAVING
EPILEPTIC FIT
      EPILEPSY IS PSYCHIC ORGASM
A CLEARING FUNCTION

    BREAK DOWN
       U
    IS   T
    BREAK THROUGH
LEADING
    TO NEW METABOLISM
WHICH MUST
INCLUDE PROVISION OF BASIC MATERIAL NECESSITIES
FOR ALL WHO ARE ON

    60,000 M./hR. JOURNEY
     AROUND
    SUN

OUR MAJOR SOURCE OF ENERGY

BIRTH CERTIFICATES OUR CREDIT CARDS
    ALLOWING FOR
TAP IN
    TO OUR NEEDED SHARE
      OF
    CONSTANTLY TRANSFORMING
POOL OF PLANETARY ENERGY

   FREEING

OUR CONSCIOUSNESS
TO DEAL WITH REALLY IMPORTANT PROBLEMS
OF
MAN'S ORIGIN
MAN'S PURPOSE
MAN'S DESTINATION

OLD CONCEPTIONS
HAVE BROUGHT US
TO THIS MOMENT

VEHICLE
CONVEYANCE
MUST BE CHANGED
AS MAN
GAVE UP WALKING
TO HORSE
BOAT
TRAIN
CAR
FLY
& THEN
SPACE TRAVEL
HE MUST GIVE UP
HIS SCARCITY FEARS
HIS OLD NATURE
MONITERED
BY ADRENAL CORTEX
FEAR
FIGHT   FLIGHT
& LEARN
THE NEW POSSIBILITIES
THAT REAL FREEDOM
FROM ECONOMIC NECESSITY
COULD PROVIDE

NEO-LUDDITE
DE-STRUCTION
OF COMPUTERS
WILL DELAY
TOTAL PLANETARY HOOK-UP
OF
ALL

INTO A SYNERGISTIC
               NETWORK
OF THOSE ABLE
           TO SHARE   **IDEOMASS**
PLANETARY   EVOLUTIONARY
        LEGACY
THAT WILL ALLOW FOR
           THE OCCURRENCE
OF COMPASSIONATE
        TRANSFORMATION

KARUNA

NOW
     HAPPENING
         AT THE EDGE OF CONSCIOUSNESS

OF
    POST   CAPITALIST YOUNG

GENE POOL
          IS SHIFTING
    UNDER STRESS
        OF TRANSITION
   ONLY
      DEEP
        INDIVIDUAL SILENCE
           &
         STILLNESS
   WILL ALLOW FOR
        THE RE-EMERGENCE
OF   **EST**
     DIRECTED
       POSITIVE FORCE
   THAT CAN STEER
EXPLODING
    TECHNOLOGICAL ENERGY

SYMBOLIC ADDICTION
     TO
     ANY PARTICULAR PROGRAMMATIC
     WILL IMPEDE PROCESS
OPENNESS

TO ALL
    FORMS
        OF THE NEW
            ESSENTIAL
IDEOLOGY
    WOULD CONSTRICT
    PROCESS
        INTO CATEGORIES
THAT DESTROY
    NEW SPIRIT

FOCUSED

    PRE-AWARENESS
  OF THIS
    WILL ALLOW
FOR REJECTION   OF ALL ATTEMPTS
    THAT NARROW
& RUSH TOWARD GOAL
    BEFORE
        PROCESS
PRODUCES
  A GOAL
        OUT OF THE NEXUS
OF ITS OWN
    STRIVING.

Discussion

FRIEDENBERG: Now it seems to me that Lipset in his comments about Marx and Engels and others was really providing further evidence in support of the main point that I was trying to make: that is that I wouldn't have expected that what I would regard as uptight effective revolutionary left wingers or whatever to dig at all the kind of trip I have been trying to get into. I think his authorities were absolutely correct in their analysis. I am sorry I am afraid that the foreign minister of the National Liberation Front is probably also right. But what I was trying to say from my point of view was that I didn't want to conceal those costs, I wanted to add them in and take responsibility for paying them, and that if insisting on the kind of freedom that did indeed grow out of privileged middle class life was going to be a drag on the revolutionary tendencies of the world, I would still do it. I do not judge all of my political aims by whether they are consistent with the world revolution or not. I think that I feel sorrier for Timothy Leary than almost anybody I could name. I do not mean that he is worse off than anybody else in the world. But I think that he must be a real aristocrat. He could not have made the kind of mistake about Eldridge Cleaver that he did make if he had not trusted people more than a person who had had less privilege would have been likely to do. I was very sorry to see that happen and it convinced me that Eldridge Cleaver will sometime be president of the United States. And I can not see any reason now why he shouldn't be.

In connection with Mr. Hentoff's comments I would want, just for the record, to point out that Ivan Illich's first trip into education came when he was a parish priest and Cardinal Spellman was Archbishop of New York. Spellman was very much Ivan Illich's protector, as a matter of fact, as long as he lived. What Illich launched was the first program of its kind in East Harlem, in which he enlisted the aid of decidedly poor, often black, Spanish-speaking youths who were not in school as tutors to teach English to other Spanish-speaking kids who did not know it. This thing was such a tremendous success that the Church almost disowned it. If it had not had support from the Cardinal I daresay that Illich and his people would not have been able to go on with it as long as they did. But it is not true that Illich's schemes immediately become irrelevant as soon as they are put into an urban setting of this kind. As a matter of fact that is really where they began.

HENTOFF: I always wondered how the late Cardinal Spellman ever made it to heaven, if he did. One word about Cleaver and then Leary. I pretend to no more knowledge than anyone else, except I knew Eldridge Cleaver, although I have not seen him since he left the country rather quickly. I think one ought to realize the situation he is in in Algeria. He is the guest of a "revolutionary" government which is a puritanical government, as is the Cuban government, which you will find out if you decide to smoke grass or be a homosexual at the

University of Havana. He was very much afraid, I think, that Tim was going to turn on a lot of people, and Eldridge is into power politics.

I found the beginning of Professor Lipset's talk fascinating because it indicates again how different people can live through the same experiences and see them as if they were different centuries. I am sure the statistics are correct about the polls that show that people over fifty saw the war was a mistake first. I just question the meaning of the word "mistake." I would gather that most people over fifty or forty meant by "mistake" that we did not kill all those gooks right off. I can not see that they saw it as a moral mistake or any other kind of mistake. Also, I am no expert on the gerontology of the peace movement, but I have been deeply into it both as participant and writer. I will grant that in 1959, at one of the first demonstrations against the war, which then consisted of a few hundred advisors, at City Hall Park in New York the average age of the thirteen or so people there were pretty high. There were Dorothy Day, A.J. Muste, Dwight McDonald; but I would not call them your average elderly Americans. But I would think that if you look back, not at the statistics but at what actually happened, at the teach-ins for example, the professors had to be dragged into them by their students. I think it is an extraordinary misreading of history to go by these polls. Thank God these polls did not exist in the nineteenth century or the eighteenth century, because then there would have been fewer historians, and who would have needed Dostoevsky to tell us what life was like in Russia because you could have taken a series of polls. Finally, by counterculture I was trying—perhaps I was not clear enough— to get beyond life style. Let me put it this way: Jerry Rubin, the way he looks, what he smokes, that's not what A.J. Muste was about. Jerry Rubin also has a tax free foundation which never gives any grants. And that is not what A.J. was about. What A.J. was about, what Cesar Chavez, Ray Mungo, and a lot of other people who are not into politics at all, are about is better illustrated by quoting Chavez. "When we are really honest with ourselves, we must admit that our lives are all that really belong to us, so it is how we use our lives that determines what kind of men we are." And if the counterculture means anything, however diverse the expressions of its lifestyle, whether it is in communes or the pediatrics collective at Lincoln Hospital in the Bronx, or whatever, that is what it's about. And I think in that sense Chavez and A.J. were indeed part of that. And I think you can go back to the early Christians; they were part of it too.

LIPSET: Allow me to make one comment in relation to Nat Hentoff's statement about my remarks. Of course it is true, it was implicit in what I said, that the peace movement, the activist component of the peace movement, were youth and were students. At least in my reading of what has happened in the last five or six years, without the campus-based peace movement, the anti-war movement, we would be even deeper into Indo-China than we are now; we would have 700,000 troops there rather than whatever the number at the moment. While we have got way too many in there now, 300,000 too many, 700,000 would have meant a very different thing and Lyndon Johnson very well might still be president of the United States had it not been for the youth base, the student base of the peace movement. But at the same time that that is true, it is also true that almost every movement, when it takes hold, is a youth movement. The Nazi movement was primarily a youth and student movement. The Wallace movement was primarily a youth movement and its most activist component, which has now gone off in almost an overt fascist direction, the National Youth Alliance, is a youth and student movement. They have a lot more energy, are a lot more idealistic. Youth are more patriotic if they are in that direction than older people of the same note and are more activistically pacifistic if they are on the pacifist end of the syndrome. So that whenever you get a movement which is a movement for change or even a movement for counterrevolution, it is largely a youth movement. Now the fact that the movement that you see in our midst is a youth movement does not mean that this is youth in general. As it so happens, there has been a very deep split in this country, not between the ages, but within the age cohorts, between different types of youth. Because the split is in part both on and off campus, and because the political activism and the counterculture both circulate in and around the campus and interact to a very heavy extent with each other, the recognition of the kinds of cleavage I am pointing to has been generally missing. And I think it's important to recognize this, particularly if one is trying to develop certain political strategies, strategies based on electoral action.

Cesar Chavez, of course, has lived up to the kind of statement that Hentoff read. But Chavez devotes himself to organizing people in trade unions. Organizing people for election. His whole life is in this direction: recruiting people for elections and recruiting people for trade unions, recruiting people for political action. The problem that various people have raised with certain aspects of the counterculture and its style is that it turns other people off. Lenin argued in the following terms, talking to young revolutionists: to be a revolutionist you have to recruit people to the revolutionary movement who are not revolutionary, who will be critical, who will not understand you, who will be alienated from you. Consequently you want to come to them, to get as close to them as possible. Lenin, who was, to take an example, a very principled and dedicated atheist, said don't go and talk about religion, don't go and talk about God. You talk about jobs, about work, about war, about peace, but it doesn't matter, if a man wants to believe in God and if he comes along with us, let him believe in God, and the same way for a man who wants to have his life style, don't bother him about sex. Lenin was very much, in terms of what he recommended to the young radicals, a puritan in sex, not because he believed in puritan sexual norms, but because he believed sexual norms at the moment were less important than political power, and therefore, if people are willing to join you on the political power issue, don't bother them, don't upset them by making them anxious about their beliefs about sex. That is, in effect, what he was saying. Now you may say that that is a very conservative view or that it reflected his own hang-ups, and certainly the country he helped to create, or the system he helped to create, is not exactly a model of a free, unrepressive society. But the tactical question, if one wants to set political priorities at a given moment (which is incidently what Madame Bihn was talking about) is, I think, the question of what about student activists who either consider themselves not political, or if they are political have a political strategy which says nothing works or you can not make effective change unless you change people. The main issue is changing people, even if it is only a minority who set an example to create a new society and a new culture within the old. That is a strategy which is obviously a defensible strategy, but it is one which I for one would conclude dooms a lot of people to live in the here and now, in conditions which could be improved if one was willing to try and concentrate on making small improvements like ending the war.

AUDIENCE: I am most interested in the link between political action and change, and the counterculture. What I would like to see discussed among you is whether the counterculture is fundamentally counterrevolutionary or perhaps has some potential to be revolutionary. It seems to me that the link between being young or having long hair and being in the counterculture and being revolutionary is very tenuous. Can you discuss that at length?

HENTOFF: We are dealing again with such an amorphous term that I find it hard to give you any kind of generalized answer. Let me try to respond to the question about whether the counterculture, whatever that may be, is possibly counterrevolutionary. One of the first things that Cleaver did when he got to Algiers was to make a film that was later shown to a lot of people in this country—Black Panther parties, cadres, other people. It was essentially an organizing instructional film. And he came on hard against dope. (This was long before Tim Leary had gone to Algeria.) In the film he said you guys are going to be infiltrated, in fact you are infiltrated. No matter who you are and what you are doing, they have three guys working eight hour shifts, twenty-four hours a day, and they are not on dope. So if you are going to be on something that makes you any more vulnerable then you already are, which is pretty vulnerable to start with, you are crazy. So in that sense, if you are in that kind of politics, then a life style that puts the kind of gratification one gets from grass ahead of what you are doing politically is not counterrevolutionary, it is stupid.

For all the Media, Pennsylvania, files have indicated about the sloppiness of the FBI in guarding their own offices, they have been appallingly effective in infiltrating all kinds of groups. One of the things that came out of the New York 21 trial was that the chief witness against them, a black undercover detective, was Malcolm X's bodyguard at the time Malcolm was assassinated. And if you remember that picture in *Life* magazine, he was the guy who was giving Malcom artificial respiration. It is kind of scary.

It is very hard for me to be specific about something like counterculture. Is rock counterrevolutionary? It depends on what people are doing and what sectors of society they are organized to move into. I don't know for a fact if members of the pediatrics collective, which is in alliance with the Young Lords, and has made a fundamental change at Lincoln Hospital, smoke grass for pleasure. I would expect some of them do. It is a slippery kind of concept to get into, and perhaps its my own Consciousness I plus II hang-ups, but I am really more concerned about the quality of people organizing, and what they do when they organize and how they link into people. There I agree with something Professor Lipset said about the necessity of starting from where other people are.

After a group of hardhats had exercised their patriotism on a number of people's heads in the Wall Street area last spring, Neil Postman and I, who are both teaching at N.Y.U., along with a group of students, decided to communicate with a group of hardhats who were working on a library there. Except for Neil, I was the most clean-shaven of the bunch. We went toward them, Neil carrying two six-packs as a kind of totem-cultural offering, and the first hour was murder, not fortunately literal, but figurative, until Neil finally caucused and said, "Will you give them the flag please, just let them have the flag, and then we can get into something that might be of some mutual use." This went on for several days at lunch hours. In fact, the guys gave up their lunch hours. It was interesting to see the stereotypes falling on the part of some people on both sides. It was most interesting to me, and this is my old style hang-ups, to see that when you get a guy who's forty-five years old being told by a young intern, "Hey did it occur to you that the average working man in Scandinavia has much better health conditions than you do, even though he makes less. Now how come?" I don't say we made an instant socialist, but there was something happening here, there was something going on that was not just rhetoric.

FRIEDENBERG: I think the whole tenor of my opening comment would make it clear that I rather think the counterculture is counterrevolutionary in its effects. I think that is regrettable, but I think it is true. The reason I think so is basically rather different from anything that has been mentioned so far, even by me. That is that I think on balance that revolutions are extremely ineffective ways of making major changes in life styles in society, that generally speaking they do not do a great deal more than cause a major, though sometimes temporary shift in elite. But sometimes not temporary. Nevertheless, it would seem to me, for example, and even though the fact of a revolution is only one of many factors involved in it, that life in the Soviet Union today is probably a great deal more like life in Imperial Russia than life in England could be like that which prevailed there before World War I. This is true partly at least because the dangers, sacrifices, and risks involved in carrying on a successful revolution, and the anger that has to be behind it to undergo such privation, are almost certain to convince you for a long, long time that the people you defeated had the best of everything. Therefore you won't really be able to examine serious alternatives to their life-style. I cannot imagine any other reasons, say, why the Russian ballet should continue to be the most old-fashioned, least innovative of any kind, when they had been in the forefront of it, other than if it was so groovy before it must still be good. What is much more important is that people who came to power had no cultural alternative, no set of tastes of their own in which they had confidence. So I think the counterculture is likely to continue to be counterrevolutionary in its effects, but more innovative than revolution.

AUDIENCE: My question for Dr. Lipset relates to what I see as a kind of pessimistic interpretation of history. Mr. Mumford sets up a kind of historical process whereby cultures have repeatedly seemed to kill themselves off. Now we have acquired a technology that is going to be the final scotching of civilization: the process is the same, but now we have tools that will do the job once and for all. Now if the *culture* has done this over and over it does not seem to be much good to make a list of *counter*cultures which have failed. If the culture has repeatedly failed, doesn't it imply we have to go outside the culture if we are going to finally come to an answer?

LIPSET: I would agree, but you may recall I started off talking about what I called pretentiously the law of limited possibilities. The thing that strikes me in this sense is how unimaginative the counterculture is; that all it is is counter, if you will. If, as my reading of various earlier forms of protest suggests, there is an enormous overlap in the practice, behavior, style, the obscenity of the means for showing your disdain for the Philistines and the bourgeoisie, it suggests that the current revolution really is terribly unimaginative and therefore does not have any new answers. It is just applying old answers; even without knowing them. It is not the same as the Marxists who repeat themselves. They repeat themselves not because of new inventions, but because they read the same books. The interesting thing about countercultural phenomena is the extent to which the identical way of snubbing the Philistines and the bourgeoisie come up simply as if saying "If they're clean so we'll be dirty." I was looking for a case where the opposite occurred and I found one limited one. That was around 1910 in Edwardian England where there was a group of very eminent students who in this period when all the distinguished men, the eldest men wore beards, were clean-shaven. This was not exactly a counterculture, it was twenty or thirty Cambridge undergraduates. But the thing of just being opposite is really being a prisoner of the establishment. That may be too strong an indictment.

HENTOFF: To use a technological word out of another milieu, there is overkill there. You say the counterculture is just counter. Granted my difficulty in being precise about what the counterculture is, I think I have some sense of individuals in it and the values they reflect over a period of time. You look at the new schools movement. Now granted this is nothing new, there was John Dewey, but the direction is different. I think it is more deeply rooted now. It is going to have all kinds of hassles, but it is astonishing the number of people who are going into learning, into helping other people to learn. I think that it is a very strong movement.

LIPSET: But that is institutional action.

HENTOFF: No. It is in and out and sometimes it is as uninstitutional as you can get. I was going to talk about the legal profession. There are a good many young lawyers going into public interest law whose life styles are pure counterculture, whatever that may mean. There are also the growth of advocacy architects and the kinds of medical interns that are coming out of the schools and working in the schools. I think there could be durable effects and I think it is the greatest oversimplification to say that it is all counter.

LIPSET: Now I would agree with that. I am sorry. You are right. I was overkilling in the sense of ignoring concrete proposals and actions which are new. What I was mainly referring to may be the tritest part of it, but it is still the thing which gets most visibly identified with it and turns some people off; this kind of personal lifestyle. A lot of that is, I think, simply counter. And the repetitiveness of it has not resulted from diffusion, but simply from looking at what "they" are like and saying, "I will be different."

EINHORN: I want to make one comment on that. Making lifestyles visible is a very conscious desire for the nature of life style is a pattern to be looked at. So that when we make our life style visible we are forcing other people to look at their life style because it is the life style of the past culture that has created that 36,000 tons of TNT per person on this earth. When we make ourselves extremely visible and put ourselves forth as images, we are asking other people to use us as mirrors. The first thing you do with a mirror you do not like is to throw stones at it, which is what has happened to us. We have become scapegoats. After awhile it began to reflect back. The media, once it gets started on one of its movements, has to go through its entire chain. It is like getting a vibration going until that vibration peters out. Hippies died a long time ago, but I have been called a hippie for the last three years. A problem of categorization. We are trying to bring also the nature of categorization to visibility. That is what the study of phenomenology is all about. We are trying to bring that back into public life. We are trying to take the great ideas of this century and make them visible.

5

Symposium on Technology and Humanism

Robert Boguslaw

I suppose that in the duel between the cowboys and the spaceship men, I am on the side of the Indians. The student chairman of this conference, Ronald Aminzade, described it as a significant attempt to approach certain fundamental questions on the nature and direction of technology and to understand and evaluate the present and potential impact of technology and technique upon the social order. The questions he suggests include: Is man in control of his future? Will the technological developments of the future result in greater freedom for man or in his eventual enslavement to or destruction by forces beyond his control? Does technology render humanistic values obsolete? And what new values are engendered by technological change? To what extent can current social tensions be viewed as a result of the inability of social institutions to keep pace with technological innovations?

These questions seem to indicate that technology holds the key to man's future. Now, I don't mean to be rude but although I applaud the sentiment behind this enterprise, I think many, if not all, of these questions are the wrong ones to be asked. In the first place, I don't think we should be asking about the impact of technology upon the social order; rather, we should be asking about the impact of the social order upon technology. I think technology is fundamentally a dependent rather than an independent variable. Moreover, we should not be asking about whether Man (with a capital M) is in control of his future. I am an incurable optimist, and it never occurs to me to question whether man will be in control of his future. Or rather, it seems to me the problem is similar to the one posed by the man who goes around saying life is rough. We really shouldn't ask about the alternative to life—we should ask about the alternatives to its being rough. So, of course, Man is in control of his future. The question is which men. And through what set of values are their futures to be controlled?

A third point about these questions: we should not be worrying about whether man eventually will be enslaved or destroyed by forces beyond his control. If men are enslaved or destroyed, it will be by other men. There are no inanimate villains these days. Fourth, technology is never neutral. It embodies a set of values of men. It reassembles chaos; it is some form of imposed order. It has always involved value choices. Sometimes the precise nature of these choices is quite obvious. More often, their nature is either latent, obscure, or quite deliberately disguised. One of the tasks of well-motivated individuals in this area

109

is to expose the precise nature of value choices embodied in various forms of technology. For example, the ABM system commits the United States to what I call a cocoon mode of dealing with international tensions. The entire range of dialogue is confined to the discussion of the penetrability and size of cocoons on both sides. The problem of peace is posed in terms of some kind of monstrous Freudian sexual fantasy on a gargantuan level in which the very notion of arms control or disarmament is experienced as a sort of castration threat or worse.

Fifth, technology does not make humanistic values obsolete. Humanistic values can be made obsolete only by anti-humanistic or non-humanistic values. Sixth, no new values are engendered by technological change. Some old values may be either strengthened or distorted. To the extent that technology redefines existing life support systems and makes them include wider configurations of transportation, communications, manufacturing, mining, and agricultural subsystems, to that extent traditional values of cooperation and concern for human need rather than individual profit should be strengthened. If these values are not strengthened, we are in the presence of a social, not a technological, pathology.

Seventh, and most important of all, we must, I feel, go far beyond the traditional activities of understanding and evaluation of all these phenomena. It is important for serious students of technology and social change to participate in social change activities. This does not mean to engage in mindless activism. On the contrary, it means to strip the gargoyles of ignorance from the outer surfaces of technology, and reveal the de facto value choices embodied in them for what they are. It involves using the intellect as a weapon in the battle against despotism disguised as technological progress. It also means organizing people to engage in the range of necessary activities to combat not technology per se but anti-humanistic technology. I would define anti-humanistic technology as any technology that embodies predominantly selfish, paranoid, or destructive values. It is not simply nuclear weapons, ICBMs, ABMs, chemical warfare agents, or biological warfare agents, but nonmilitary technologies proposed mainly for purposes of pride or profit rather than for human dignity. Time and circumstances are always relevant to any consideration of action *vis-à-vis* technological development. Space exploration, for example, as such is not anti-humanistic; it becomes anti-humanistic when it absorbs resources needed for sick and hungry children and adults. Automobiles are not in themselves anti-humanistic; they become anti-humanistic when their manufacturers refrain from engaging in the technological development work necessary to insure that their pollutant potential is eliminated or significantly reduced. They become anti-humanistic when persons who profit from their sale succeed in holding back the development of mass transportation systems that would make large numbers of them unnecessary and would make thousands of acres of concrete deserts or highways unnecessary. Again, the SST is not anti-humanistic as such. It becomes violently anti-humanistic when it is seen as an alternative selected because of narrowly chauvinistic reasons. It is an alternative which not only promises to result in greater noise and air pollution, but one that represents a serious diversion of energy, skills, and other resources desperately needed in other areas of social life. Again, this is not to say that technology is neutral; but rather that we must consider time and the special circumstances in which it is introduced as relevant facts. So at this conference, on Technology and Social Change, I say let's focus on social change. Technology is part of the social process, and will change only when broader social changes in fact take place.

Melvin Kranzberg

The modern novel, the contemporary drama, and today's poetry have as one of their most insistent themes the fear that technology is taking over from man. And, in this current literature of anti-technology, two metaphors constantly appear: Frankenstein's monster, from the nineteenth-century thriller by Mary Wollstonecraft Shelley, and the robots from Karel Capek's play of the 1920s, *R.U.R.* Both these metaphors engulf us in a blood-chilling speculation that man has created the mechanical means of his own annihilation, either literally or figuratively.

These metaphors are more apt than the critics who use them realize. For one thing, the Monster of Frankenstein and Rossum's Universal Robots were created by men who sought to do good for mankind. To quote Dr. Frankenstein, "I thought that if I could bestow animation upon lifeless matter, I might in process of time . . . renew life where death had apparently devoted the body to corruption." Frankenstein thus conceives of himself as man's benefactor. as one who will "pour a torrent of light into our dark world."

The engineers who manufactured Rossum's Universal Robots were also motivated by altruism. As Harry Domin, general manager of the robot plant, states:

In ten years Rossum's Robots will produce so much corn, so much cloth, so much everything, that things will cost practically nothing. There will be no poverty. All work will be done by living machines. Everybody will be free from worry and liberated from the degradation of labor. Everybody will live only to perfect himself.

At this point, our anti-technologists go off the track. While willing to admit that technologists are motivated by altruism, they imply that the creations turn against their creator because there is something wrong with technology. If they would remain true to the letter and spirit of their metaphors, they would discover that it was man himself who was responsible for turning these technological creations against humanity.

The Monster of Frankenstein—and I am speaking here about the original novel—sought only warmth, understanding, and sympathy. Yet his gruesome form and appearance turned people against him, until finally, out of despair, he turned against mankind.

In the case of Frankenstein's monster, it was not the machine which failed, but human beings, including Dr. Frankenstein himself. Herman Munster, the lovable oaf of the television series, was truer to Mrs. Shelley's original novel than was Boris Karloff in the movies.

In the play *R.U.R.* it is also a human rather than a technological defect which creates problems. The trouble is caused, we learn, by Dr. Gall, Head of the

Physiological and Experimental Department of *R.U.R.*, who changed the composition of the robots and sought to make them more human—by making them more irritable. Only when the robots ceased to be machines and became more human did they become dangerous.

The story of Frankenstein is a psychological thriller; the fault is not in the monster created by man but in man himself. *R.U.R.* is a modern parable, an indictment of selfish materialism, not of the machine. It is important that we remember this distinction, that we do not allow our modern literary Luddites to stampede us into unthinking criticism of technology by literary allusions that are incorrect.

For the fact is that technology, far from dehumanizing man, is actually an instrument of civilizing man. Indeed, it has been one of the prime elements in the creation of civilization. All of us—even those who deplore it—recognize that, by calling ours a technological age. It is called that, not because all men are engineers and certainly not because all men understand technology, but because we are aware that technology has become a major disruptive as well as creative force in the twentieth century. But man has always lived in a technological age, inasmuch as his life and culture have always been bound up with his technology.

Indeed, man himself is a product of technology. Anthropologists seeking the origin of mankind have attempted to differentiate between what constitutes "almost-man" and the genus "man." The chief distinction they can find is that man employed tools. Man as we know him probably could not have evolved or survived without tools—he is too weak and puny a creature to fight nature with only his hands and teeth. The lion is stronger, the horse faster, the giraffe can reach higher; tools served as extensions of man's hand and amplifiers of his muscle power, enabling him to adjust his hereditary organic equipment to an almost infinite number of operations in virtually any environment.

It is not surprising, therefore, that many anthropologists define the human species on the basis of tool-using and tool-making, or to be more exact, tool dependency. Modern physiology, psychology, evolutionary biology, and anthropology all combine to demonstrate to us that *Homo sapiens* (man the thinker) cannot be distinguished from *Homo faber* (man the maker). Indeed, we now realize that man could not have become a thinker had he not at the same time been a maker.

Not only was technology basic to the emergence of our species, it played a major role in the beginnings of civilized society. The development of settled communities, the beginning of what we call civilization, rested upon a technological innovation, agriculture. We do not know exactly how or when agriculture began, yet once men discovered that they could cooperate with nature by sowing seeds and waiting for nature to perform the miracle of growing crops, there arose the possibility of settled and civilized life.

Unlike the hunter, the agriculturalist could not live in constant conflict, but had to cooperate not only with nature but with other human beings. If he spent all his time in fighting, he would have neither time nor energy for carrying on agricultural pursuits; yet if he ran away from his enemies, his crops would go untended and he would lose his livelihood. With the coming of agriculture, therefore, the beginnings of civilized society emerge, and along with it man's dawning awareness that he must live and work together with others if he is to survive.

From savagery to barbarism to civilization, man's material progress throughout the ages has been bound up with his technology. The story of technology is a story of man's attempt to control his environment: in terms of materials, from stone to bronze, from bronze to iron, and iron to steel; in terms of energy, from human muscle power to animal, to wind and water, to steam and oil, to rockets and nuclear power; of machines, from hand tools to powered tools, to mass production lines, to computer-controlled factories.

Despite the role of technology in the panorama of human history, we frequently come up against those who regard technology as something divorced from the essence of humanity. The humanists ask: What is human about a monkey wrench, a lathe, a computer? What repels them about technology is the very "inhumanity" of its objects, for example, the monster automatons which it has created and which threaten to make man expendable, or the "anti-humanity" of its by-products, such as the pollution which threatens our environment.

It is true that we ordinarily think of technology as something mechanical, yet the fact is that all technical processes and products are the product of the human creative imagination and human skills. The story of how man has utilized technology in order to master his environment is part of the great drama of man fighting against the unknown. Man has long sought to use nature to his own ends, to master the environment, to control nature. This is a very human activity—this is technology.

Furthermore, the significance of technology lies in its use by human beings. Take, for example, the telephone. If we regard it only as a collection of wires through which current passes from a transmitter to a receiver it would seem to have little interest, except for telephone technicians and repairmen. But the significance of the telephone lies in its use in transmitting messages. It is the communications function of the telephone that gives it importance, and the function of technology is its use by human beings.

Technology is inseparable from men and communities. The technologist is concerned with the applications of science and other forms of knowledge to the needs of man in society; he is up to his neck in human problems whether he likes it or not. When our Peace Corps builds a road in tropical Africa, this road is more than an exercise in civil engineering. It is, in fact, a major experiment in social anthropology, for it affects the primitive villages up-country and acts as a communication link which will stimulate the acculturation of these people to modern Western society.

But technology is responsible for much more than the evolution of our species, ministering to our animal needs and creature comforts, and setting powerful social forces in operation. The cultivation of the humanistic arts—literature, music, poetry, drama, painting, sculpture—would have been almost impossible without technology. These require leisure for their exercise, and this leisure is only attainable when men have provided—with the aid of technology—for their basic needs of food, clothing, and shelter. Technology, by enabling man to do more than subsist, has made possible man's cultural development, as well as his social and political evolution.

All well and good, you say. But look at the inhuman uses of technology. What about the devastation wrought by wars throughout history, and the present possibility of destroying the human race through nuclear warfare? What about the deterioration of the environment, created by air and water pollution, the spoliation of the countryside, and the rot of our cities? Is not technology responsible for these also?

Yes and no. Ironic as it may seem, the fact is that these deleterious and dangerous applications of technology also represent its human use. Regardless of the causes of war, the fact is that rifles do not fire themselves any more than did bows-and-arrows in earlier times, and that missiles are guided by electronic devices made and set by human beings. The history of mankind shows us that war, like technology itself, is a very human activity. Whether we go to war for self-preservation or mom's apple pie, or for abstractions such as religion, the nation, or a distant neighbor's freedom, these represent human motivations.

In a sense technology is Janus-faced. It can be used for both good and evil purposes; while the intentions of some men might appear evil to us, they always appear justified to them. War, unfortunately, frequently represents the human use of technology for the sake of inhuman purposes.

But, you might argue, war represents a special case. What about the harmful effects of technical applications which were designed for peaceful ends? What about the smog which befouls the atmosphere of our cities and which is gradually making them unlivable? Or what about the indiscriminate use of DDT, threatening the ecology of entire regions, so that man poses a threat not only to his fellow humans but to all other living creatures?

I submit that these cases, like war, also represent human uses of technology. For the sad fact is that all of us applaud technology when we can utilize it for our own profit or pleasure, but few of us worry whether these applications of technology might be harmful to the community as a whole.

Let me take a case close to home: pollution of the atmosphere caused by automobiles. This is what is known as a threshold phenomenon. That is, a smaller number of automobiles have little effect upon the salubrity of the air; however, when a sufficient number of automobiles emit noxious fumes, these reach a point where they can no longer be dissipated into the atmosphere and where they pose a threat to the health of the entire community. For purpose of illustration, let us say that 100,000 automobiles can operate in Philadelphia without creating a health hazard, but the 100,001st automobile's exhaust fumes push the amount of noxious emissions beyond the threshold of safety. Now, who is responsible for the dangers created by the automobile smog? The 100,001st car or the other 100,000? Are any of us willing to forego the convenience and pleasure of having our own individual transportation in order to reduce the smog level? No, it is always the other fellow who should leave his car at home and walk or use public transportation, not us. We are willing to accept the risks of a smog-laden atmosphere for the sake of our own comfort and convenience. We place the blame not on ourselves, and our own selfishness, but on Detroit for seducing us to buy vehicles which give off dangerous emissions. We continue to drive our cars and angrily demand that Detroit change the engine design in order to do away with the dangerous exhaust. In other words, we rely upon the "technological fix," that is, remedying matters by the application of more or better technology rather than our own forebearance. We favor our own inhuman use of technology in order to suit our own comfort and convenience—and we ignore the health and safety of the community at large.

Or, let us take the case of DDT, which is now being banned by our government, and which seems a classic example of the heedless application of a scientific technology without thought of eventual harmful effects. But I submit that the case of DDT is not so simple. Let us remember that it was employed for worthwhile human goals: raising agricultural productivity and eliminating disease-carrying pests. Now we find that DDT has done not only that, but also threatens ecological systems. So, belatedly, we decide to ban DDT. We can afford to do so, for our high technological level enables us to use alternative means of pest control to achieve the same results at a slightly higher cost. Other nations, however, are not so well placed. Poorer, underdeveloped countries must make use of any and every technological advance which they can afford in order to subsist, even if that technology might have harmful side effects. For example, it would not be economically feasible for India to change to an insecticide less persistent than DDT which would require spraying every few weeks instead of twice a year. Yet India must have the insecticidal benefits from DDT despite its harmful effects. Its use there has cut down the incidence of malaria from 100 million cases a year to only 15,000 cases, and the death rate from 750,000 to 1,500 a year. In more advanced industrial countries with higher standards of health, malaria presents no such problems. Thus, while some applications of technology might seem harmful to us, others perceive them as a blessing. Which is the human and which is the inhuman use of technology?

But perhaps we are asking the wrong question. Instead of trying to show that every application of technology responds to some human need or want, even if these may sometimes be very narrowly conceived in terms of individual or special interest groups, perhaps we should be asking whether or not technology has a dynamic of its own? To put it another way, is there a technological imperative which human beings are unable to control? Certain philosophers of our times, such as Jacques Ellul, think so. They claim that society is at the mercy of its technology, which determines our actions and institutions. This is an old complaint; over a century ago Ralph Waldo Emerson said, "Things are in the saddle and ride mankind."

We have a current example that seems to prove Emerson's adage: the SST, the supersonic transport. To most of us, there is no very pressing need to cross the Atlantic in three hours rather than six, or to go from Los Angeles to New York in half the time it now takes. Yet a few years ago our government decided to invest large sums in developing a supersonic transport. Many critics complained that the technological imperative was at work: because we had the technological capability to build the SST, we proceeded to undertake the task without concerning ourselves with the human or social gains to be derived therefrom. But let us not blame technology for our own selfishness. Aerospace corporations envisioned profits from the SST; economists pointed out the financial benefits to be gained by selling the SST to foreign countries, thereby helping take care of the balance of payments; and patriots justified the SST simply because we must not fall behind the Russians or the British and the French, who are also building supersonic transports. While few of us would benefit directly from the huge expenditure of sums for the SST, certain interest groups would have derived profit and pride from it.

It would seem that the question, then, is not whether our technology is controllable by man, but whether men are controllable by man. Machines are not designed, built, and operated by other machines. Behind every automaton I see the face of a man. Or, rather, many men: the engineer, the scientist, the corporation executive, the government bureaucrat—all of them seeing how their own interests might be served by further applications of technology.

And let us get one thing straight. These are not evil men. They do not intend to harm the community. Far from it! Instead, they are convinced that pursuit of their own special goals will somehow benefit mankind as a whole.

Let me give you an example of this in terms of electronic bugging devices, which many people have denounced as a threat to human privacy and hence to human freedom. Does that mean that the scientists and engineers who designed and built these devices are cunning Machiavellians, the "mad scientists" of movie fame who wish to control the world? Nonsense! Indeed, I scarcely need convince this audience that the typical technologist is the soul of naive innocence.

But let us take a brief look at just how the typical engineer views certain technical matters which others might perceive as having dangerous social consequences. Did the scientists and engineers who replaced the martini olive with a tiny radio transmitter think of destroying human freedom by eavesdropping on private conversations? I am certain that the question, as it presented itself to them, was a simple technical problem, namely, how to miniaturize an electronic device. If they thought at all about the possible consequences of such miniaturization, they probably thought that it would be a boon to mankind by making hearing devices smaller and less obtrusive so that hard-of-hearing people would be spared the embarrassment of unsightly and unwieldy hearing devices. But then somebody hit upon the bright notion of using these miniature devices to bug cocktail conversations, thereby depriving the martini of an olive, the martini drinker of his privacy. Hence we blame our engineers and scientists for depriving us of privacy when all they really sought to do was to solve a technical problem.

If engineers and scientists are not totally responsible for the misuse of their work, who is to blame? Should the blame be put on the politicians, the generals, the businessmen—each of whom is really doing his own thing? Perhaps the blame rests not on individual men or groups of men, but on the human institutions which we have developed for control and use of our technology.

Indeed, one of the oldest conflicts in human history is that between the individual and society. Social institutions control and use our technology. One characteristic of institutions is that they are created and run by people, and consequently, they tend to serve the interest of their owners or managers rather than that of their constituency. Hospitals are run for the convenience of the doctors and the staff—how else are we to explain the fact that patients are awakened at 9 o'clock in the evening to be given sleeping pills? Banks are run for the convenience of the bankers, not the depositors—how else can we account for their being closed just when it would be most convenient for the depositors to do business with them? Outside of Spiro Agnew, who really believes that corporations are run for their stockholders, insurance companies for the insured, unions for their members, political parties for the voters, or universities for the students?

Institutions are run for the convenience and benefit of those who control them. Though they sometimes war on each other, their most pernicious habit is joining forces with other institutions to reinforce each other. Technology serves as a means whereby some of those who control institutions can expand their power further. Are men or institutions to blame?

In effect, this is the dilemma faced by John Stuart Mill when he endeavored to delineate the individual's rights *vis-à-vis* the demands of society. The battle has long been joined between man and the institutions of his own creation. Science and technology have merely changed the battleground, weapons, and dimensions of this age-old and never-ending struggle.

The conflict between the individual and social institutions points up the fact that our society is composed of institutions and that all people are under the authority of some large organization or many different organizations, both public and private. When we ask if men can control their own institutions, several questions immediately arise: (1) to what extent are these institutions answerable to society as a whole; (2) to what extent has technology determined the size, scope, and nature of these institutions; and (3) how can the individual make his will known within the institutional matrix?

The answers are not simple. Yet we must seek for them if we attempt to answer the question of whether people can control technology, for it is evident that they can do so only through control of the institutions which themselves control technology.

In contemporary American society two powerful sets of institutions stand out: the federal government and the corporation. And, if we listen to our social critics, neither of these giant sets of institutions are very responsive to human demands and social control.

According to Adolf A. Berle, some 500 giant corporations hold in their hands the great bulk of American wealth; and according to John K. Galbraith, these giant corporations control their own environment and immunize themselves from outside control mechanisms. The corporation emancipates itself from stockholder control by separating ownership from management; by brainwashing its customers, it insulates itself from consumer sovereignty or the dictates of the marketplace. It also puts pressure on a compliant government to assure a market for its products by guaranteeing full employment, to eliminate risks by generous guarantees of loans, to subsidize investment in research and development by government grant and contract, and to assure the supply of scientific and technical personnel required by the modern technostructure.

Government itself, as our young leftists are always telling us, also seems immune to outside pressures, except those coming from the military-industrial complex. It is insensitive to public need and social demands.

In a sense, technology is partially responsible for the growth of giantism in corporations and government. The growth of big government and big business—and the concomitant big science—are perhaps inevitable in a highly complex and interdependent society, made so by scientific-technological developments.

The scale and pace of life in an industrialized and crowded society require that men be organized in order to get anything done, and this in turn requires a scale of operation beyond the ability of any single individual. In brief, it requires a bureaucracy. Our problem, then, is the sensitivity of the bureaucracy to social demands and to individual needs.

In his book, *Red, White, and Blue,*[1] John William Ward describes the conflict between the American ideal of individual character and achievement and the American penchant, indeed, genius, for building organizations. There is no irreconcilable contradiction between these two. The problem is not the existence of institutions, for that is a given fact. The question is whether we can make existing institutions responsive to the individual, or if we can forge new institutions which will be responsive to the individual and responsible to the common weal.

Institutional practices are not sacrosanct. They have changed throughout history and will change in the future. As Garrett Hardin has pointed out, what might have seemed moral a hundred years ago—for example, the disposal of waste into the nearest river—is immoral today because the accumulation of such singular acts results in polluting the water supply for a complex urban society. Similarly, values are not sacrosanct. More recently, Harvey Brooks has pointed out how our values have changed within the past decade. Enumerating a list of national goals as of 1960, which included such things as getting a man to the moon, he discovers that we have successfully fulfilled many of these goals through the aid of science and technology; but we are still unsatisfied, because by 1970 the goals had changed, partly because we had fulfilled some of them.

The question, then, is not whether technology controls people or people control technology, but whether people can control institutions which in turn control technology and society, and whether our institutions can be made sensitive to the value changes occurring in our society.

When the late William Fielding Ogburn spoke of a "cultural lag," he meant that institutions, behavior, and values lagged behind our scientific and technological potential. Now "culture," in the form of changing values and scientific and technological capacities, has moved far ahead of our institutions. These lag behind the new norms and values which are being formulated by the younger generation. Science and technology have given us the potentiality to feed, clothe, and shelter all our people, but the older institutions of a free enterprise society have kept us from achieving those ends. Rather than making such elementary needs and wants into a basic right and then doing still more to enrich human life, we allow our institutions to control our technology for narrow or selfish ends.

We no longer need measure progress in terms of how many manufactured articles people own, how many destructible weapons our nation possesses, or how many space vehicles we can deposit on celestial bodies. The new norms are abundance and health for all, and life as a satisfying development of human potential and interpersonal relationships.

Hence the new question which we must ask is whether technology, in its institutional matrix, can be directed toward the satisfaction of human wants and toward meeting reformulated social norms. I think that it can.

For one thing, we are aware that the major questions regarding the control of science and technology are not scientific and technological problems, but human and political questions. We recognize that advancing science can bring problems, disturbances, and dangers, as well as benefits. We recognize also that science and technology have given us powerful new tools to meet society's changing needs and desires, and we are beginning to recognize that these powerful and better tools demand a better, more highly skilled, and more careful "carpenter."

I suggest, too, that we are beginning to think about the mechanism by which society can control the heedless or unbridled applications of science so as to serve the expanded needs of a crowded earth and with due thought about the world which we plan to leave to future generations. One of the most hopeful of these mechanisms is what is known as Technology Assessment, and the recent vote on the SST shows us a primitive and imperfect form of Technology Assessment at work.

Technology Assessment came into public view in response to the need to curb the selfish use of science and technology, whether by individuals or institutions. It came into being when we recognized that the application of science is too important to be left in the hands of engineers, scientists, businessmen, generals, government bureaucrats, or any groupings of individual or institutions seeking only to promote their own narrow goals or interests.

I am particularly aware of the dangers involved in allowing scientists and engineers to determine the use of their own work. Despite the valiant efforts, stretching over many years, of those of us who have been teaching the humanities and social sciences to embryonic scientists and engineering students, the fact is that scientists and engineers have remained politically innocent, socially unaware, and ethically naive. And, parodoxically, they are also corrupt, because they submerge their own professionalism in order to serve as loyal hirelings of institutions which use science and technology for narrow ends and purposes.

But science and technology have too many ramifications in our modern world for us to allow any portion of the population or any group of institutions, including governmental institutions, to utilize them to serve their own interests without consideration of the common good. In a democracy, such decisions must be left to the political process, where, hopefully, the welfare of the community as a whole and of the many conflicting interest groups in a pluralistic society are consulted. The control of society, and of technology as part of that society, should rest upon all of us, not only upon our technocrats.

I think that the time has now come when decisions regarding the applications of science and technology must be made by the community at large rather than by special interest groups. This does not mean that I subscribe to the cliché that "there is nothing as powerful as an idea whose time has come." That may be powerful rhetoric, but it is bad history. Anybody can name several ideas whose time has long passed, but which have exhibited little power. Notable among these are the concepts of world peace and human brotherhood. They have been around for some 2000 years, accepted in theory but never in practice.

Now, however, democratic decision making regarding the applications of science and technology—a process involving Technology Assessment—strikes me as an idea whose time has come, and I think it also has the power. It, too, is a matter of the human heart, but it also has some powerful hardware and interest behind it. We know now that scientific developments have a broad and accelerating social impact. We know also that we have the scientific and technological capabilities to perform different tasks in many different ways, so we need not settle for a technique which might have harmful long range effects. We have the knowledge, wealth, and opportunity to apply science and technology for the benefit of mankind.

What really counts—and the examples of world peace and human brotherhood plague us on this point—is our willingness to apply that knowledge in practice. In other words, the decision is up to each of us—and to all of us—as to whether we wish to allow our science and technology to serve a set of obsolete and narrow values or whether we wish to control them for the benefit of society as a whole.

Notes

1. John W. Ward, *Red, White and Blue: Men, Books and Ideas in American Life* (New York: Oxford University Press, 1969).

Charles R. Dechert

Our symposium is concerned with Technology and Humanism. I take this to mean a consideration of the impact of science and technology on the human condition and its implications for the satisfaction of human needs and for the intellectual, moral, emotional, and spiritual growth of persons, both as individuals and in the community. I shall take as my point of departure not only the extraordinary capabilities of modern machinery to produce goods, but above all our increasing ability to process information, to plan and program future events, to control our natural and human environment.[1]

It may be said that man's total environment is increasingly an artifact. During the last few years such economists as Barbara Ward and Kenneth Boulding have popularized the concept of "spaceship earth"—that is, the earth as a closed system, a total environment within which a single human community and its individual and group members live and work and pursue their destinies. Man's total environment consists of a physical or natural environment and a human or social environment. The history of technology, as conceived up to now, has largely been concerned with the development of man's individual and group control over the physical environment; the development of weapons for hunting; selection of cereal crops; the domestication of animals; mineral extractive and refining techniques; methods of food preparation; methods of building, and methods of clothing men. Closely allied to the development of physical techniques was the development of social techniques; the farm as an institution, communal structures, military organizations, the *polis*, to name but a few. Karl Deutsch and his associates' analysis of social science "breakthroughs" since 1900 recently published in *Science* would indicate an increasing level of social invention, and concomitant potential for control of the human environment.[2]

Clearly there is an intimate relation between control of one's physical environment and overall environmental control. The human community exists or subsists by extracting and transforming the wealth of the earth to satisfy human needs and desires. The early period of modern technology, the paleotechnic era, to use Lewis Mumford's term, was largely concerned with the physical transformation of nature and the multiplication of goods. The new technology provided or permitted by the use of high speed computers is concerned with the rational organization of technical processes and their control. Computer programing the stages of industrial production, the use of mechanical and electronic sensors and effectors, computerized decision units to automatically adjust line production units, are all quite widely used. Computer applications to agricultural production include farm management services that optimize utilization of the soil in terms of crop mix or a mixture of crops and animals, and least-cost preparation of feed mixes. Food processing and transport between farm and consumer is increasingly a function of computerized planning. So is the manufacturing process, the minimizing of transportation and storage costs, and rational and high return distribution techniques.

As we move from the actual production of goods, either in the factory or on the farm, to the transportation, storage, and distribution of goods, we move from the realm of the social environment. We should recall, however, that even the natural environment is increasingly a product of man. The present concern with pollution illustrates this. The air and water of our cities are often contaminated. Rivers and even the high seas suffer from industrial wastes and petroleum residues. On the positive side, flower gardens and green belts, parks and game preserves, the layout of farm and forest with the opportunities they provide for domestic animals and wild life, the distribution of housing—all of these create or modify the natural environment in such a way that nature itself is almost an artifact. There have been indications for many years that the multi-variant problems of meteorological prediction and control may be on the way to solution.

The extraordinary logical capability of the high speed computer has been applied to many areas of the social environment: (1) personnel and recruitment information systems; (2) automated patent search; (3) "reading" texts for content analysis; (4) teaching factual material at all levels from grammar school to college; (5) storing and analyzing stock exchange data; (6) printing; (7) simulation in virtually all areas: business management, military strategy, marketing, political and economic development; (8) navigation systems; (9) space and class scheduling; (10) inventory control; (11) medical diagnoses; (12) psychological test interpretation; (13) documentation systems and archives; (14) preparation of indices and concordances; (15) preparation of mental case histories; (16) tax accounting and analysis of tax returns; (17) land, sea, and air traffic control; (18) computer aided design, including architectural design; (19) warranty systems; (20) billing; (21) land use determination; (22) guidance systems of all types; (23) control of ticketing in mass transit system (with implications for on-line real time data processing of consumer demand for transport to regulate transit schedules); (24) market research of all kinds, including art; (25) banking procedures and accounting of all types, including the "credit card revolution" made possible by the computer; (26) organization of the "over the counter" stock market; (27) crime information systems, etc.

In brief, the organized rationality made possible by the high speed digital computer is providing us with an increasing social control capability.

Personalization

Many fear that the extensive application of system analytic techniques and computer capabilities to handle large amounts of data for the organization of social systems will result in a depersonalization of man and of labor. I think that the reality is probably the opposite.[3] The depersonalization of men that occurred in the paleotechnic era was due precisely to the replacement of the extraordinary flexibility of human minds with a horribly simplified and mechanical rationality. Let me explain.

Both military operations and industrial operations require programing future events, that is, organizing sequences of interrelated actions or events over future time in such a way as to achieve a given end result. This is basically what is involved in factory organization. The modern military staff was developed as an instrument for such planning in large scale military operations. One difficulty of such plans was their complexity and mechanical nature. Too late it was discovered that once the mobilization plans produced by the general staffs prior to World War I were put into motion, all possibility of recall or change was lost. Without being aware of it, political leaders who had made decisions to mobilize, perhaps as an exercise of political-diplomatic pressure, found that their mobilization was irreversible. The troops could not be released, or their scheduled movements to the frontiers halted without creating an intolerably serious threat to the national security. World Wars I and II are perhaps the most telling and horrifying examples of men caught in a mechanistic social machine lacking reason or conscience that senselessly destroyed them on the Somme, at Verdun and Stalingrad. Rapid data processing capabilities, however, increasingly permit the organization of complex sequences of future contingent interacting events in a manner that permits rapid readjustment of the plan to either unforeseen events or policy changes. The programs at various levels of social organization can themselves be programed at a higher level, permitting the overall organization of complex decentralized activities possessing a high degree of autonomy.

Social Values and Social Planning

The paleotechnic era brought the brute mechanical simplicity and the primitive logic of early machinery to the organization of the factory. As Peter Drucker has pointed out, the analysis of a job into its components does not necessarily mean that the individual worker must perform all day and all his life some minute repetitive operation.[4] Interestingly enough, it is precisely these minute repetitive operations which are being abolished today by automation and cybernation. Work is increasingly concerned with a control of complex processes, programing industrial operations, and the maintenance of equipment. These can be very interesting jobs indeed. Similarly, the primitive model of an economic system found in Manchesterian economics constrained most men to the brutal impoverishment brought on by markets in which labor was considered a commodity. The so-called natural laws of economics were nothing more than an abstract, more or less arbitrary, and highly simplified model of the social universe. This model was imposed by public authority and the police power regardless of traditional cultural or moral values. Today it is perfectly possible and indeed normal for us to interfere with the working of free market in order to achieve other values such as price stability, or full employment on the national scale. Increasingly it should become possible to intervene effectively at a community level.

Appropriately structured social and economic policies, tailored to the local level, could probably be designed, if it were thought socially desirable, to restore the artisan, small businessman, and farmer to an honored place in our society. Do these social statuses really help develop such traditional virtues as thrift, industry, stability, reliability, conscientiousness, and independence? If so, assuming the desirability of such value orientations, can the environment be so organized that their restoration in a substantial portion of our population becomes likely?

The individual producer's inadequate resources and inadequate control of environment have left him the prey of personal misfortune, the business cycle, and large economic aggregates whose control of resources material—human, financial, and increasingly informational—have provided an inestimable competitive advantage. The community might organize itself so as to provide a certain social insulation to its artisans, merchants, farmers, and service people, while modern data processing techniques could help make them quite efficient producers in small and local markets.

The richness of our information environment may well help do away with a rigid hierarchical type of organization which has characterized the military, big business, and big government up to the present time. These too have created a psychological effect of great, inhuman and overwhelming machines.[5] As men move from the mechanical repetitive tasks better performed by machines to positions requiring initiative and judgment, as jobs are replaced by roles in the overall community, there is a corresponding need for a far higher degree of intimate and organic interrelation within both the socioeconomic and the political communities. Communication in a hierarchical sense will tend to be replaced by dense webs of communication—probably by the provision of increased facility for interpersonal contact.

The increased leisure based on our production technology implies an increasing capability for the active participation of all in the life of the community. The development of interpersonal relations and affective webs not only gives greater meaning to life, but can help insulate the individual against the arbitrary exercise of increasingly concentrated economic and political power at the national level. Central files having extensive data on every individual exist throughout the society. At the national level extensive dossiers are held by the Federal Bureau of Investigation, the Internal Revenue Service, the military services, the Bureau of the Census, the Labor Department and the National Science Foundation; by schools and colleges, the Educational Testing Service and similar agencies, insurance companies (auto, life, medical), medical data centers, banks and credit agencies, professional associations. Biography publishers like Marquis also have extensive dossiers. Apparently data is often exchanged among such agencies, and is, of course, potentially available to persons in agencies that process or do computer work for such repositories.

On the other hand, such repositories have potential for personalizing and enhancing the effectiveness of society. Let me illustrate. In the late spring of 1970 it became apparent that a serious problem had developed regarding full employment of scientists and engineers, primarily as a result of cutbacks in defense research and development and in the aerospace program. According to a news report in the March 12, 1971, issue of *Science*, there are presently some 60,000 unemployed scientists and engineers, not to mention those trained in the social sciences.[6] Most of those recently graduated from universities at the Ph.D. level are unable to find academic positions. Among the older members of this group the human effects of such unemployment can be devastating, economically, socially, psychologically, and professionally.

The Department of Housing and Urban Development and the Department of Labor are planning to employ some 400-600 unemployed scientists and technicians and eventually expand this to 2,000. Legislation proposed in the Senate by Edward Kennedy and in the House by Representatives Robert Giaimo and John W. Davis would appropriate some 450 to 500 million dollars over a three year period to finance retraining programs, provide grants to small businesses, fund research and planning of conversion programs, and establish nonprofit community corporations which would hire unemployed professionals and put them to work on domestic programs. These are essentially piecemeal programs. Obviously any effective effort to eliminate the overall problem must work not only in terms of employing single individuals, but in terms of some grand design sufficiently comprehensive to incorporate all of the suggested programs. Present information-handling techniques make possible such a system. Frankly, it seems to me that the present availability of highly qualified scientific and technical people presents us with an unprecedented opportunity for the beginnings of a massive reorientation of intellectual effort into new areas of national concern. The research systems engineering and administrative skills developed in the aerospace and defense effort could prove highly relevant to newer areas of research that involve environmental quality and environmental control in the broadest sense. A committee print of the Senate Committee on Interior and Insular Affairs provides an analytic scheme indicating the breadth of this concern (Fig. 5-1). This breakdown can be tied to existing agencies and programs of the federal government.[7]

The National Science Foundation's Register of Scientific and Technical Personnel includes social security numbers. It should be possible to machine match these numbers with posted tax withholdings, when a scientist or engineer no longer has withholding tax paid, one recognizes his potential availability. I have been informed by knowledgeable Internal Revenue Service people that this would be quite legitimate under the present laws. Now in many cases such a person would be going into business for himself or would be in the process of

128

Figure 5-1

Classification of Activities Within the Scope of Environmental Management

I. Renewable Resources Conservation

A. Pollution control:
  1. Air pollution control
  2. Water pollution control

B. Agriculture:
  1. Agricultural production research and assistance
  2. Agricultural soil conservation

C. Water resources conservation:
  1. Water supply
  2. Water quality control
  3. Saline water conversion

D. Land management:
  1. Public land use management
  2. Watershed management
  3. Forestry research and management
  4. Wetland and estuary conservation

E. Marine resources conservation:
  1. Oceanography
  2. Commercial fishery conservation

F. Atmospheric sciences:
  1. Basic meteorology
  2. Weather modification

G. Space exploration and research:
  1. Space research
  2. Space vehicle construction and operation

II. Nonrenewable Resources Conservation

A. Urban land utilization:
  1. Urban planning
  2. Urban redevelopment
  3. Urban public recreation
  4. Utility engineering and construction
  5. Zoning

B. Nonurban land utilization:
  1. Surveying and mapping
  2. Rural community stabilization, planning, and development
  3. New city planning and development

C. Transportation:
  1. Urban transit planning and development
  2. Highway planning, safety, and beautification
  3. Air transport planning and development
  4. Marine and inland waterway transport planning and development
  5. Traffic control and safety
  6. Railroad regulation and safety

D. Energy:
  1. Thermal-electric plant siting, design, and operation
  2. Electric power transmission line siting, design, construction, and operation
  3. Fossil fuel exploration, inventory, and research
  4. Heat utilization and dispersion
  5. Nuclear power research, development, and operation
  6. Hydroelectric power research, development, and operation

E. Mineral resources conservation:
  1. Mineral exploration and inventory
  2. Materials research and development
  3. Solid waste storage, recycling, and disposal
  4. Mining technology research and development
  5. Mineral extraction research and development

III. Environmental Health and Well-Being

A. Physiological health and well-being:
1. Sanitation
2. Radiation control
3. Industrial and domestic health and safety
4. Environmental health protection
5. Contagious disease control
6. Pest control
7. Food and drug regulation
8. Flood control
9. Natural disaster warning and relief
10. Population control

B. Psychological health and well-being
1. Noise suppression
2. Relief of acoustic, mechanical, and interpersonal tension stresses
3. Promotion of community identity
4. Population dispersion
5. Environmental education

IV. Promotion of Amenities

A. Outdoor recreation:
1. Public recreation, planning, and development
2. Wild lands preservation
3. Sport fish and wildlife conservation
4. Conservation and promotion of natural beauty

B. Cultural stimulation:
1. Urban beautification
2. Historic preservation
3. Enhancement of architectural and engineering design
4. Maintenance of continuity of environmental associations
5. Provision for diversity of experience and life style

V. Ecological Research

A. Human ecology:
1. Basic research in human ecology

normal transfer of employers. This could be determined informally by a telephone call either to the erstwhile employer or the person himself by an officer of his professional association. If such a person's availability is confirmed informally he might be contacted through his professional association to be put on a part-time consultant basis. As a consultant he might discuss and generate, write or review project proposals in the national interests. It has been my experience that most senior people, if motivated, demonstrate extraordinary fecundity in thinking up Research and Development proposals.

Normally I should think that proposing scientists would play a major role in implementing approved, placed, and funded proposals. Substantial numbers of second level professionals, technicians, and workers would obviously be brought in for project implementation. Hopefully at least a fair number of projects would be chosen to have a social payoff and commercial or industrial spin-off. The point that I'm trying to make, however, is that a proposal of this type, implying the use of sophisticated computer facilities, can bring about a personalization of the employment process. It can help tailor jobs to the individual. It can help arrange for highly skilled people to do their thing in self-generated projects in the public interest.

It has been suggested that the present administration is interested in setting up placement facilities for scientific and technical personnel on a decentralized basis. Apparently many have been thinking of decentralization in geographic terms. In the foregoing proposal there would be a *functional* decentralization. NSF or the National Academy or someone else at the national level, the central governmental level, could provide a matching capability. Contact and professional activity would be decentralized functionally through the various national organizations and very possibly through their regional and local branches (Fig. 5-2).

Personalization can be achieved through the use of old-boy networks. I think it's been the experience of most of us in professional life that after a few years we develop rather extensive networks of contacts within our fields. Some of my own research has indicated that scientific activity tends to take place in basic information exchange groupings of from ten to a hundred people. At a certain point in the growth of a scientific enterprise it tends to perform mitosis and divide into two or more sub-specialties. Members of these specialties and sub-specialties can often be identified through the use of Selected Dissemination of Information Systems—who is reading whose material? Many, if not most of a relatively small group reading one another's material are almost certainly personally acquainted. On a national scale it would be possible to identify networks of interpersonal relations by simply analyzing the source and destination of telephone calls, local and long distance. (In the early 1950s this method was suggested for identifying nodal persons in the decision and internal information exchange structure of the Defense establishment.) I suggest that such a technique could be used to identify nodal persons in the scientific social

Figure 5-2

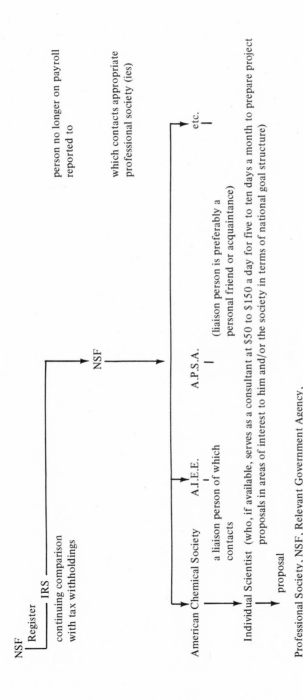

structure or indeed in the national social structure and that personal acquaint-
ances could be used to bring members of the scientific and technical community
back into constructive work. Notice that I suggest using these people on a
consultant basis so that they do not lose status or self-respect. Again it is my
personal experience that a man paid $700 for seven days consulting during the
course of a month might very well spend 20 or 25 working days on his task.
Scientists have roles, not jobs.

Such an effort would try to employ men at their highest skill levels in terms
of their knowledge, or their innovative capabilities, or their critical capacities. At
the highest ability levels they would be put to work producing work for others
so that there would be a human multiplier effect that answers the needs of
society. I strongly suspect that putting our top talent to work in innovative
activities would have a substantial impact upon the general unemployment
situation in the United States.

Education and the Community

Computer techniques may well tend to individualize education. Biographic data
on the student, his personality profile, data relating to perceptual skills,
memory, and learning ability, motivational structure, and interests, plus complete data on achievement to date will permit a tutor to set tasks of reading,
action, and research on an individual basis, adapted to the student's level and
capabilities. The tutor will be able to assess the results of this instruction with
immediacy. For rote, routine, and factual learning, teaching machines and
programed instruction can replace the teacher in many repetitive chores and free
him for constructive activity and personal contact. As library facilities are
automated, not only books and documents, but also films should become
increasingly available for educational purposes. In turn, curricula can be
individually tailored to student interests, abilities, and needs. This should
increase opportunities for developing creative personalities by greatly increasing
the possible combinations of instructional inputs into the student population. In
brief, the ideal of education envisaged by Robert Hutchins may not have been
feasible, owing to the technological limitation of the time and may only now be
coming to be a possibility.

The educational applications of modern data processing equipment extend far
beyond making available documentary and other instructional materials, and
providing the learner with analytic instruments. The computer also permits the
use of very sophisticated simulation methods for the development of attitudes,
values, decisional, and perceptual skills. Simulation can be used to instill both
operative habits and orientations in terms of a reference model of personality.
Simulations can be used, for example, to develop the behaviors and value
orientations that make for competitive efficiency in a modern industrial

economy. This approach may well permit us to program rapid cultural change—even to achieve a net separation in certain critical behaviors between one generation and the next. The desirability of such procedures, and the limits of their application are ethical questions having implications for the long term development of all mankind.

The perennial question of the Greeks was *ti e paideia?* What is education? The question is no less basic for us. What sorts of people do we want? And how shall they be formed? In a sense the "new Soviet man" is a reference model. Such innovations as the nursery schools are an effort to create an environmental field in which the personality traits and skills associated with this reference model will be developed. In some sense, of course, John Dewey created the reference model of the modern American, the democratic personality which our school system tries to create.

Clearly there is need for constant feedback from the real world to test the effectiveness of the educational system in molding character, personality, and skills—and further feedback on the effectiveness of the character, personality, and skills so created in coping with the environment and in achieving personal and social excellence. It is entirely possible that in this area, as in so many others, a certain pluralism is desirable—that is, the creation of a multiplicity of personality types and a wide variety of skill combinations. To some extent the American system of higher education achieves precisely this.

Long range rationality in the social system requires first that we increasingly clearly define our goals in terms of each level of social organization: What sort of a people we wish to be and what do we want in terms of material and cultural and spiritual goods? Second, it requires that we analyze the capabilities of the living population, the potential changes of those capabilities over time, and project our human requirements in terms of these factors. The overall system must be patterned to accept the limitations built into a population. Perhaps one answer would be to so organize the structure of the overall universe of jobs (or roles) at given future times so as to provide interesting and challenging activity within the skill capabilities of all of the members of the population. This might very well mean reversing a present trend and increasing at least temporarily the projected proportion of relatively unskilled work. In terms of its human objectives the future society might very well be characterized by a substantial increase in the number of gardeners and lawn keepers, persons providing personal services and custom production of the artisan type.

As early as the 1930s it was suggested by Alexis Carrel, in *Man the Unknown*, that the growing complexity of modern society and the rising amounts of scientific information available will increasingly make necessary the early selection and almost life-long training of persons of very high talent.[8] Again, the computer and centralized data on ability and personality, collected by such organizations as the Educational Testing Service and Science Research Associates, permit the identification of outstanding talents coming from all sectors of the population. The provision of appropriate intellectual, moral, and emotional training will develop the talent of these citizens for the public enlightenment and welfare as well as their own personal fulfillment.

Notes

1. Many of the concepts suggested in this study were suggested in a paper prepared for the Symposium on Comparative Administration and Management Systems sponsored by The Society for General Systems Research at the annual meeting of the American Association for the Advancement of Science, New York, December 1967.

2. K.W. Deutsch; J. Platt; and D. Senghaas, "Conditions Favoring Major Advances in Social Science," *Science* 171 (Feb. 5, 1971): 450-59.

3. This position is also taken by Alvin Toffler, *Future Shock* (New York: Random House, 1970), Part Four.

4. See Peter Drucker, *The Practice of Management* (New York: Harper, 1954).

5. See Lewis Mumford, *Myth of the Machine: The Pentagon of Power* (New York: Harcourt-Brace, 1970).

6. *Science* 171 (March 12, 1971): 985-87.

7. Daniel A. Dreyfus, "A Definition of the Scope of Environmental Management," prepared for the Committee on Interior and Insular Affairs, U.S. Senate, 1970.

8. Alexis Carrel, *Man the Unknown* (New York: Harper, 1939).

Ashley Montagu

I have been wondering what has become of the subject of human
these discussions. Since I've not had the good fortune to attend th
meetings I don't know whether anyone in them defined technology,
humanism. But then, definitions, as you know, are not properly mea〳   ⌣⌣⌣ at
the beginning of an inquiry. They can only become so at the end of one. So I
hope that by the end of this panel, we shall all know what we have been talking
about: which is a confirmation devoutly to be wished, but seldom realized. The
ideas to which I'm going to address myself are best illustrated by a piece of
history that occurred some years ago during a strike in that city so much given
to strikes, namely New York. This time there was a strike of the keepers at the
Bronx Zoo, during which a much valued chimpanzee escaped. And after a
sedulous search for him lasting some four days—since he was a very highly
intelligent and amiable creature—he was eventually found in the lowermost
stacks of the New York Public Library. In his left hand he was holding a copy of
The Bible, and in his right hand he was holding a copy of Darwin's *Origin of
Species*. And when asked for an explanation of the meaning of this, he meekly
replied, "Well I was simply trying to discover whether I'm my brother's keeper
or my keeper's brother." This, I think is the essence of the living situation. I say
living rather than human, because I think that it is extremely important for us to
realize, particularly in a culture in which we have been told to multiply and
increase and subdue the earth, that we have to understand that if we're going to
talk about such things as humanism, technology, or anything else that human
beings are involved in, we must include in this the whole of animate as well as
inanimate nature. It is, after all, a total respect for the total environment which
is essential if we, as human beings, are to survive. We are not the lords of
creation. We are so far from being the lords of creation that I can tell you from
intimate communion with plants and animals, and stars and streams, and rivers,
and lakes that man is the worst blight that this earth has ever suffered. The
blight is not human beings, but people. Our problem is that we have made out of
potential human beings—people. Just as, for example, the church has made
millions of Christians out of potential followers of Jesus.

It is perhaps necessary to point out that man is a creature who is constantly
more in danger than any other living thing on this Earth. As a consequence of his
unique and peculiar evolutionary history, he has become the most educable
creature on this earth. And this, along with our egomania, means that we are the
most intelligent creatures on the face of this earth. For example, Dr. Kranzberg
properly referred to the Linnean classification of man as *Homo sapiens*. And
described him, I think, as the thinking creature. *Homo sapiens*, man the thinker.
Well, the wise guy, *Homo sap*, very definitely, but certainly not *sapiens*. The
wisdom is there as a potentiality, but it has to be earned. Oscar Wilde remarked
of this definition, it is the most prematurely, oafishly arrogant definition ever

offered of a species. And we are, of course, always awarding ourselves these accolades and presenting ourselves with all these Congressional Medals of Honor, and putting ourselves at the very top of the ladder of the scale of nature, and regarding all other creatures and all other living things as inferior to ourselves. But as a consequence of this peculiar ability for learning more than any other creature is capable of learning, man has not become the most intelligent of all the creatures on this earth, but the most confused. This is because he is a creature who is not only capable of learning more sound things than any other creature, but by virtue of his educability, of learning more unsound things than any other creature. Which is something we scarcely ever think about. But when you put the unsound and the sound together, you don't get intelligence, you get a state of confusion, the state that most people are in.

The fact is that we have far departed from the understanding and the meaning of humanity, as a consequence principally of our love affair with things, with technology. Dr. Kranzberg has referred to the Industrial Revolution. The first Industrial Revolution was undoubtedly the discovery of tools, the second Industrial Revolution was the discovery of fire, the third Industrial Revolution was, in prehistoric times, the discovery of agriculture, and the fourth the development of urbanism. That's long before our middle of the eighteenth century Industrial Revolution and its nineteenth century galloping development. With the discovery of agriculture, man started on that rapid descent toward dehumanization, which we are now in the midst of. Man as such has evolved over a period of five million or more years. During almost all of that long period he was a food-gathering hunter. As a food-gathering hunter, man lived in small populations of forty or so individuals. This represented some half dozen families, usually with not more than three children each. Everyone knew everyone else, everyone was involved in everyone else's welfare. Man continued to evolve as part of a long 78 million year continuum of the evolution of all mammals into a state of increasingly profound relationships. This constituted an entirely new zone of adaptation, namely adaptation through the learned part of the environment, whereby man made his decisions on the basis of the traditional wisdom handed down by his ancestors and elders. Everyone knew everyone else. Everyone was aware of the fact that he must be involved in not only every other human being's welfare, but in every plant, and every animal. And therefore he never went around exhausting the animal population or the water population or the plant population. He knew that he was related to everything in the Universe, the clouds, the sky, the constellations, the stars, the planets, and so forth. But the important thing is this, that man has evolved from a vegetarian, whose ancestors spent 78 million years in the forest, to a creature who now has to adjust himself to a totally new world in which he becomes not only a food-gathering hunter, but a hunter who is increasingly dependent for his survival on his tool-making and upon his hunting, and who knows that whatever he does virtually at every moment during his life will effect everything else on this earth. One may still study this among the remnants and relics of such populations, who are still food-gathering hunters who we have not completely destroyed, although we are busily engaged, of course, in doing so at the present time. The point I wish to make is that as a consequence of this involvement in the welfare of the other, there was a preferential selection for genetic constitutions which were endowed with the capacities to behave in such a way toward others. In short, there has been a high selection in the human species for the ability to relate oneself cooperatively with love to all others, not only to human beings, but toward everything on this earth.

With the discovery of agriculture, man could control the reproduction of plants and animals for the first time in history. This enabled him to enlarge his population to very considerable numbers. In a small hunting population you cannot maintain many people, so you don't have many people. You actively engage in birth control by abstinence. With the increase in the numbers of a community, such as occurred in the Middle East between the Tigris and Euphrates, where agriculture almost certainly was discovered, for the first time there could be concentrations of hundreds, even thousands, of people. And for the first time there would develop specialization of occupations, professions, and also for the first time, the unique phenomenon of one individual being able to pass another and not know who he was and not even care. This happened just about 10,000 or so years ago. With the enlargement of these communities into urban communities, this situation was exacerbated. And, indeed, as Dr. Kranzberg pointed out, man's love affair with technology began in this period.

It is not true today that there has always been a technological age. The difference between man in the technological age and man in the food-gathering hunting stage is that tools for the latter were instruments, and nothing more nor less than such. In a technological age, it is people who are instruments or are the objects of technological instruments and it is people who are made into technological objects by other people. So it is not really as Dr. Kranzberg suggested a question simply of is it technology that controls people, or do people control people. It amounts to the same thing. It depends entirely upon your view of a human being. As an anthropologist I can tell you with complete certainty, by which I mean the highest degree of probability which attaches to a particular judgment at a particular time, that man is on this earth to live as if to live and love were one. What is love? Love is simply the ability to relate yourself in such a manner toward others that you not only confer survival benefits upon them, but you do so in a creatively enlarging manner. And by creatively enlarging manner I don't mean that you send him to school or college and he goes through the higher three Rs or the lower three Rs, and the degrees by which he intellectually dies, and spiritually dies. Not at all. I mean by the ability to love in a creatively enlarging manner, the ability to enlarge the capacities of others into trained abilities in such a manner that they can continue to do so to all other creatures on this earth. So that they can then live with and love all others. This is what the humanities should be about. This is what humanism should be about. And this is what technology should be about. Technology in the service of man, not man in the service of technology.

Discussion

AUDIENCE: I get the feeling that I've been insulted by coming to a national conference, and instead of hearing people talk on very sweeping issues, like the year 2000 or the new Renaissance man, as I think has been the general tenor in past conferences, this afternoon I've just had a lot of petty textbooks definitions thrown at me. I think the reason why we all enjoyed Mr. Montagu's speech was that he talked about quasi-cosmic things like love and life. I mean instead of talking about the way computers are going to be as common as telephones in the next forty or fifty years, why not talk about the post-industrial state. For example, what will be the impact of a three- or four-day work week on America? And what about the rest of the world? What is going to be the impact of the green revolution on the developing areas of the world? I don't fault any specific remark by anyone, because what they said is all true. I'd just like to hear something a little more grand in scope.

DECHERT: In my paper, I was, in fact, talking about a post-industrial society; a situation in which the total need for agricultural and industrial production would involve perhaps 20 percent, 25 percent of the population. I was not speaking only of the multiplication of computers, but in view of the fact that we have become a highly integrated nation, this is extremely significant. We have telephone lines going into virtually every house in the country. We have been tied together in a network. We have capabilities of analyzing this network in terms of the interpersonal relations that are involved. We have developed technologies which permit a repersonalization of relations. And I think that this is significant. For example, a good deal of our development up to now has been in terms of plugging people into a social machine. You study at the Wharton School of the University of Pennsylvania so that you can enter the business community. Most of our scientists and technologists are trained to fit into the structure. It's only in this generation that the level of welfare is sufficiently high that we can begin to look beyond material remuneration toward human development. I would suggest that we may very well be moving away from a money economy. If this is true, then it is tremendously important.

One of the points that I left out here was that perhaps one answer to our current concern would be to so organize the structure of the overall universe of jobs or roles so as to provide interesting and challenging activity for the skill capabilities of all the members of the population. This might very well mean reversing a present trend away from jobs and roles having increased skill and toward increasing, at least temporarily, the projected proportion of relatively unskilled work in order to achieve society's human objective. You might have a future society characterized by a substantial increase in the number of gardeners and lawn keepers, persons providing personal services, and custom production of the artisan types. Now the chap who goes out with a Ph.D. and goes into making leather shoes in Georgetown is following this sort of prescription. And the society and its present technological capabilities have made that sort of personalization or humanization possible.

MONTAGU: But the question is, is that humanization, and I think that the criticism made is a perfectly justified one. That we're talking in textbook terms. For example you, Dr. Dechert, mentioned Alexis Carell. Well this, if I may say so, shocked me profoundly. Alexis Carell's book was published in the 1930s and was called *Man the Unknown*. It was complete rubbish at the time, and it was not surprising that when the Spanish Civil War occurred, Alexis Carell went around collecting money in order to fund Franco's forces. And it is not surprising that he ended up as the Minister of State in the Vichy government, and died in an Allied prison. So I think that it's a very unhappy choice of authorities, both in this connection, and in others. Now what I think our critic was saying is why don't we get down to the basic issues? Instead of talking about the personalization of depersonalized persons in Georgetown, or elsewhere, we should ask ourselves, "What on earth are we on this earth for?" We should ask simple questions like that. They're not complex questions.

AUDIENCE: It was mentioned earlier that technology is allowing culture to advance in today's time and I want to take issue with that. We should look at the culture that's evolving around us and look at it as a reflection of man in the technological age. And what we see is the garbage of an Erich Segal, the intellectual confusion of a Saul Bellow, or the despair of a Samuel Becket. Only rarely are we allowed the blessing of an occasional freak like Dylan Thomas. What I'm referring to is kind of decline in the technological age of what Abraham Maslow, who is kind of my model of twentieth century humanism, referred to as the B values: love, beauty, justice, courage, growth, and freedom; and of what William Faulkner referred to as the old verities. And that is what I was hoping would be the subject of today's symposium. I agree with Dr. Montagu that there has been too much talk about technology and not enough about humanism, and what I would like to know is what kind of prognosis do you people up there have for the future of these B values or old verities in the twentieth century. And what about the role of the social scientist in this dilemma? I fear that most of the social sciences are more influenced by technology than humanism, as evidenced by the very largely deterministic and atomistic types of theories and research that go on today.

MONTAGU: As Yeats put it, "The best lack all convictions, while the rest are fools of passionate intensity. The center does not hold." What we have to realize is that if we are going to change the world, we've got to change it where it begins—in ourselves. The world is not an abstraction. Our country, our nation, is not an abstraction. It is a reflection of ourselves. And we are responsible for the

mess that we are in. No matter who or what made us what we have become, this does not for a moment relieve us of the responsibility of making ourselves over into what we ought to be. And unless we do that, we cannot change the world. And when you ask what role the social scientist should be playing here, well you quoted one very magnificent social scientist who departed from traditional studies. In contrast to the abnormal, pathological, and irrelevant matters which formed the center of research by psychologists of the old school, this one man, Maslow, did begin to study healthy people. I wish the medical professional would begin to study healthy people, and be interested in health rather than in disease.

There is in the behavioral sciences a great body of knowledge available which can be taught and upon which we can pattern our lives. If we want to know where the information is, there are books available. I've written two classics on the subject. A classic is a book that is either out of print, or unread, or never read, never was read, or may be in print and is still unread; in that sense I regard my two books as classics.

AUDIENCE: Would you identify the books for us?

MONTAGU: Well, one was published in 1955. It was delivered as a course of lectures at Harvard called *The Direction of Human Development.* The other one which preceded it was called *On Being Human.* Now I seldom see a reference to these books in the behavioral science literature.

AUDIENCE: Well, I shall look for them. I was wondering if any of the other panelists would direct themselves to this issue.

BOGUSLAW: I'd like to say one thing, I find it very difficult to disagree with Mr. Montagu. He's a very determined man and he has expressed himself in favor of love and I think that I'm in favor of love, and I'm in favor of man as well as the flowers and the stars. I think that one of the difficulties with dealing with the problem at that level of abstraction is simply that it tends to obscure a great many relevant social issues. I would agree with you that most of conventional social science does not deal with this directly. Certainly in my own field, sociology, as it has been developed in this country, I would agree that, by and large, the burden of respectable sociology has not attempted to come to grips with the kinds of problems we're trying to come to terms with here. But I think that you'll find that there is a new thrust that is developing, the thrust which says we must look not at man in the abstract, but at men and particular groups of men. We must do the hard work of understanding which men in particular benefit from the kinds of conditions we live under. And this is not going to be done with flowery phrases or witticisms. I think we've got to come to terms with understanding the difference, for example, between a General Motors continuing to deal with the problem of making pollution and creating the kinds of environment we have, and the kinds of guilty feelings that many of us have about the little bit of smoke that comes out of the back of our own cars. I think we have to start isolating the particular groups of people, who are causing this, and not blame man in the abstract for the problem.

AUDIENCE: I was wondering if there were any methods by which we could be certain that people are trained to learn how to love and to think and to understand themselves. Does Mr. Montagu have any ideas?

MONTAGU: Well in the first place, they need to discontinue our so-called educational system because they're not educational systems at all. They're instructional systems. And the schools are training the three Rs and the colleges in the higher three Rs, namely, remedial reading, remedial 'ritting, and remedial 'rithmetic. And then if you have the misfortune to be conditioned in that land of perpetual pubescence, namely California, you are exposed to the lower three Rs namely Reagan, Rafferty, and the Regents. And since one of the supreme values in the United States is quantity, needless to say you would be flattered that you had ten campuses with 27,500 students on each campus, and the more the better. Now we don't have any education. Education is training in the art, the practice, and the science of love, of how to be a mench, of how to relate yourself warmly and creatively toward other human beings. If it isn't that, its technology. And that's what passes as education in our so-called educational institutions. It's instruction. It has nothing to do with education whatsoever.

We don't have the kind of institutions that go with humanity. We have the kind of institutions which go with anti-humanity, which go with technology. And, needless to say man is the only 150 pound, non-linear servo-mechanism that can be wholly reproduced by unskilled labor. And most parents are unskilled in the most important of all the arts and sciences, the making of another human being. And the way you do this is not by pedanticism, but by having teachers who are human beings. The greatest gift that a teacher can give to his students is his own personality, and the teacher who cares for his students is the only teacher who ever teaches. The care of the students begins with caring for the students, with the care of the child. And those are not just witticisms or flowery words.

Love is a tangible thing that I can hold in my hand. I can show you 100 X-rays and I can give them to you and say show me the difference between the fifty children who have been loved and the fifty who haven't. And you, who have never read an X-ray in your life before, will be able to see the difference in the structure of the bones. In one group the bones will be that of a child who has differed in only one variable from the others, namely the quality of the love that he has received. That's what I mean by being tangible. And it's biochemically analyzable, it's no longer a word that one hears on Sunday morning. Remember the meaning of a word is the action it produces.

MODERATOR: Dr. Kranzberg would you like to respond to the last question?

KRANZBERG: I detect here a dichotomy constantly being proposed between technology and man, with which I disagree. Because technology is an instrument and creation of man. And, as a matter of fact, I am somewhat puzzled again by Dr. Montagu's nostalgia for the prehistoric times where life was probably as Hobbes describes it: nasty, brutal, solitary, and short. I think that technology gives us the opportunity to worry about love and human relationships in a way in which other people in pre-industrial times did not. Let us not forget that for most of human history, the bulk of mankind lived on the subsistence level. Their major problem, the thing which concerned them most, was just how to get enough to eat in order to live on to the next day. Our industrial society enables us to worry about things such as how students relate to professors, parents relate to children, how this audience relates to the panel, etc. Now I think that technology has given us the opportunity to worry about human love and these various things in a way which hasn't been possible before.

MONTAGU: On the other hand, Dr. Kranzberg, my studies indicate to me that technology has completely obfuscated any understanding of the meaning of love and prevented or, at least, impeded us from considering and thinking and reflecting about its meaning. And as for nostalgia, well I don't want us to go back to that kind of life by any means. But I would say this: I would rather be a prehistoric or primitive illiterate man who knew that my fellows and my other animal fellows and plants loved me and I them, than a very learned professor who didn't understand the meaning of this.

BOGUSLAW: I would just like to say one thing. Speaking for myself, I can't imagine a more worthwhile goal than universal love. I really think this is the ultimate goal for all of us to follow. I think the problem of the pathology of our society, as we see it, is that it does not allow the expression of love. But I just can't accept something called technology as the villain of the piece. I know something about technology and I've never seen a computer build itself. I've never seen an atomic bomb build itself, I've never seen a bit of anti-humanistic technology build itself. These were not built by men in the abstract, they were built by men. And if we want to approach the condition of universal love, we have to look at the men who are now inhibiting that search. That is where we begin.

MONTAGU: I couldn't agree more. Dr. Boguslaw's point must be constantly emphasized. It is people who make technology. But one must also realize that technology frequently serves as a model for other men by which to make other people. This is a very real danger and it has certainly been accomplished in the western world for a great many centuries. I regard most people as sort of computerized technological artifacts who seem to have been formed by this kind of pattern. And this is a great tragedy because the greatest of all tragedies on this earth lies in the difference between what this creature was capable of becoming and what he has been caused to become.

AUDIENCE: There's a writer by the name of Theodore Sturgeon who's promulgated a law of human development that goes something like, 90 percent of everything is crap. Now I think that this is more or less obvious to the casual observer, but what I've often wondered is how do you save the other 10 percent.

DECHERT: Well, I'm not sure I can answer the question about how you protect people and individuals in society and how you resist the onslaught of junk. I think that it's essential that we realize, however, that we are part of this enormous social reality and that we cannot totally withdraw from it. And this, I think, is part of the beginning of wisdom. You may be against it, you may not want to cooperate with it, you may reject many of its values, but it's virtually impossible to withdraw from it. You have to realize its existence and that you're within it somewhere.

Secondly, you suggest that it is not enough for people to subsist with their reality and yet so many really feel that to be human is a kind of ultimate accomplishment. One of the most unpleasant experiences I think I've had was in encountering a rather senior person in the governmental structure, who had the distinct feeling that the United States would be much better off if it had 50 million people, rather than 200 million. And this wouldn't have been so bad, except that this chap was rather closely related to nuclear weapons.

It strikes me that a good many of the questions really being asked here are essentially theological questions. Dr. Boguslaw has hit upon the problem of values, whether these be non-theological humanistic, Judeo-Christian humanistic, Buddhist humanistic, or what have you. Values have to do with fundamental questions, such as why you're here, what you should do here, how you should behave. Virtually all religions, of course, would maintain the law of love. Making this concrete in a modern complex society can be very difficult. A concrete example of love in a technical society might involve a very coldblooded guy in the automobile industry, who picked up a telephone one day and called a designer and said, "Do you realize the implications of the instrument panel design you have submitted? If this goes into production, two hundred people are going to die unnecessarily next year." Would this be an act of love? I think it would.

KRANZBERG: I infer from what the questioner had to say and from what somebody else said earlier about people reading Erich Segal and Saul Bellow instead of Abraham Maslow and others, that there's sort of an elitist view of culture around here. That the notion is that we have to have the high culture and be against technology because it allows for a mass culture which is not to their liking. It is true that we have given people more leisure with our highly advanced technology, and they do not always use their leisure to recreate themselves as Aristotle would have had us do, but for recreation in front of the boob tube. I've been referred to as a learned professor without love, but I have enough love for my own fellow man to let him enjoy his own debased pleasures as he will.

AUDIENCE: I did not say people should read Samuel Beckett instead of Saul Bellow. I like Saul Bellow quite a bit. My point was that culture, as reflected in our society, is deep in confusion and despair. And that says something about the society we have in the technological age.

Bob Theobald, in the opening speech of this conference, talked about a possibility which is called guaranteed annual income. And I'd like the panel to try to come up with their own individual view on what the guaranteed annual income would do to humanism and to technology.

BOGUSLAW: Bob Theobald happens to be one of my very favorite people. I think that the notion of his guaranteed annual income stems from a very deep concern with what I've been referring to as values of some men versus values of other men. I think the problem that we face in our society today, stemming partly from the advance of technology as it is being utilized, suggests that what we have to do is change our value structure so that it does not become necessary for a person to establish his own utility within a productive system in order to be fed, and clothed, and sheltered. Now the guaranteed income as a concept, as a practical embodiment of a set of humanistic values, is in the kind of direction in which society has to move. I think what's happened, as in the case of so many other contexts, is that people like Nixon and Agnew and Reagan and Rafferty have taken some of the words of the guaranteed income and sort of mal-adapted the thing so that it reads like some sort of distorted welfare program, and I think that that's unfortunate. I don't think that's humanistic. But certainly within the context of the kinds of concerns that Bob Theobald was addressing himself to, I think this is making an awful lot of sense and I would certainly prescribe one myself.

AUDIENCE: It was mentioned earlier that technology has been associated with images of Frankenstein or universal robots, and I just wanted to say that for me, Dr. Dechert conjured up an image more like that of Alphaville, where the citizens live in a community which has a gigantic computer complex as its center. Regardless of intentions, it strikes me that a person's control over his own life is very much a basic human value and a society composed of citizens who lack this control over their own destiny is going to be subject to psychological problems that you haven't begun to discuss. I'd appreciate it if you would.

DECHERT: You recognized what I was driving at. I feel much better than I did. The fact is that these technologies do exist, and although I'm not making a value judgment on them, I think that we should be aware of the existence of all the possibilities so that appropriate social action can be taken to counter the dehumanizing elements that are implicit in, among other things, an interlinked telephone net having a hundred million terminals. In terms of the computer center, I believe there is one in Columbia, Maryland. I have been approached on a number of occasions with respect to questions of computer community design, and I've resisted this. I find it quite unattractive. The whole business of integrated documentation is dangerous in terms of the interference with personal privacy, and I think that this is the real question. As a political scientist I get worried about access to sensitive information, even medical information, by whomever wishes it. They're already talking, with liberalized abortion now here, that, in all probability, there are still going to be substantial numbers of illegal abortions performed for people who want to remain anonymous. Remember there was a movie and a play, *Detective Story*, that revolved around the loss of anonymity by a person in such a situation. I think that this is a very serious issue: the possibilities of social control that are involved if there is adequate knowledge of personality values, habits, and so forth. So that the person has only a tremendous illusion of freedom. This is something that I think everyone is conscious of: how much of his information environment is a function of conscious plan, how much news is made for effect. So I'm in complete agreement with you.

As to the personalization of education, there's been a great deal of talk about this on campuses. Now what I suggested was a concrete approach to highly personalized education. But what this involves is a tutorial arrangement in which you would be assigned material that would permit you to pursue your own interests under someone who was an expert in the area.

KRANZBERG: This is a comment on what was just said. I noticed that the speaker prefaced his remarks by saying that a basic human value is control of one's destiny. As an historian I simply want to point out that this is a fairly recent value in terms of the panorama of human history. For most of history, except for a few highly placed individuals, people did not have control over their own destiny. Their destinies, their status, was limited by their birth. Their horizons were limited. They performed the same work in the same place as their ancestors had done, and in the same way. And I think that an advance in technology has had something to do with the larger number of options available to us in terms of social mobility and mobility in space and time. And we do have larger control over our destiny. We no longer feel that we are in the hands of the gods or we have control over our own destinies only after we die, by whatever graces were uttered to us here on earth.

MONTAGU: I think the essential question here is, "What does one do about realizing one's own destiny?" Each of us is a unique individual and this should be the wealth of the human species, as indeed it can be. Because it is in the differences, not alone in the likenesses, that this wealth lies. Therefore, each individual should be regarded as a creature, no matter what his genetic limitations may be, who, by virtue of his uniqueness, has first of all the right to the achievement of that uniqueness. Second, anyone or anything that stands in the way of his development of that uniqueness must be considered criminal. This is the greatest crime that one can commit against another human being: to deprive him of his birthright, which is development, and to deprive society, which would be the benefactor of it. And therefore, the individual who has the advantages of living in a society such as described by Dr. Kranzberg is the one who has the freedom to make of himself what he ought to make. And remember that freedom is not the liberty to do what you like, but the right to be able to do what you ought. And what you ought to do is develop as a warm loving human being who helps others to develop similarly. Therefore, you maintain your integrity as a human being, no matter who laughs at you, who ridicules you, who condemns you. You must be yourself. And if we, each of us, would be true to ourselves, we would by this means solve most of the world's problems.

AUDIENCE: I see you all as humanists, I see us all as human beings and, as such, I'm surprised to find that during the course of this conference, with the exception of Mr. Theobald and with one or two members of this panel, the whole other area of the expression of human creativity aside from technology, namely the arts, has been sorely neglected. I'd like to see each of you men address yourself to this area of human creativity and to what creativity actually means in man.

MONTAGU: Well, let me say that I regard all creativity as nothing more or less than involvement. What is talent if not involvement? Again, no matter what your genetic limitations are, there is nothing to prevent you from realizing that art and the aesthetics is a very necessary and important element of life. The necessity of beauty is something that a human being should always be aware of, and not necessarily have to take courses in. But he should live his life aesthetically, and his own life should be the greatest of all the works of art of which he is capable. This of course would also assist him to grow and develop in any form of art that he chose to make his own.

DECHERT: I would just like to say one word on that. I find it very difficult to perceive people in Vietnam and in other places pursuing a creative life. I think one of the conditions for creativity is, in fact, to remove the barriers to creativity which so much of our current socially organized systems provide. So that I would say that creativity can only arrive when you've cleaned up some of these other problems of society, including the kinds of problems which persist and which are based on a kind of Social Darwinism: a view which is essentially selfish and which is anti-humanistic with respect to the broader social configuration.

AUDIENCE: That confuses me because if we're going to wait for some time in the future, how are we going to get to this solution?

MONTAGU: The future is made by what you do now, and therefore you must do what you ought to do now.

Summary of the Small Symposia

Eight small symposia were conducted during the conference, providing an opportunity for interested persons to participate in the discussion of selected aspects of the general theme of Technology and Social Change. Perspectives ranged from the highly scientific to the occult. The style of the leaders ranged from facilitator and expert resource to conventional lecturer, with questions being entertained from the floor. It is not the purpose of this chapter to recapitulate all the points of view expressed in the symposia, nor to take a position with respect to the substantive debates which occupied many, but rather to summarize the main ideas concerning the most critical issues raised during the course of the discussions.

As a whole, the seminars made clear that technology has been, is, or soon will be fundamentally transforming the condition of our environment, the structure of our institutions, the forms of our culture, the organization of our personalities, and even the very nature of our biological organisms. The impact of the industrial revolution and the revolution of technology on the farm has been to transform the United States from a rural, agricultural to an urban, industrial society. Farming and hand manufacture have declined in relation to machine production and services, and for most people the place of work has shifted from the family farm, shop or store to the corporate office or factory. The notions of the job as the new social role constituting the link between the family and the economy and the role of the husband as the family breadwinner have come into being. Extended families have broken up as people migrated to the cities in search of work in order to make money to purchase needed goods and services in the expanded cash economy. The extended family has been further weakened by the social mobility available to participants in the new industrial economy.

The symposium on "Technology and the Family," led by sociologist Charles Thrall of the University of Pennsylvania, discussed the above development as well as topics such as the impact of household technology on changing life styles and on the division of labor in the family; the desirability (both from a moral and psychological point of view) and practicability of designing different institutional arrangements for the socialization of children and for improving the quality of life for the individual (particularly women, adolescents, and the aged); and the possibilities and consequences of re-organizing the institution of work in our society.

As the pace of geographic mobility has increased, even stable urban neighborhood communities have yielded to apartment living and instant suburbs. The material and psychological insecurity created by the separation of work from the family and the consequent dependence on impersonal employers concerned primarily with organizational efficiency rather than job security or worker satisfaction has been exacerbated by the intrusion of machines into work tasks formerly performed by men. The fear of technological unemployment (which is not to deny that technology has also created a great many jobs) has been a constant concern of organized labor. Private corporations have grown enormously in size and influence; and the federal government has grown along side, often serving and occasionally restraining their expansion. More and more of the nation's people and resources have been subsumed under the supervision of an increasingly powerful centralized federal government.

An increasing division of labor has led to greater occupational specialization and a more complex interdependence between companies engaged in the different phases of production and marketing. Within the bureaucracies of private industry, and to a lesser degree public administration, specialists or technocrats have risen to positions of influence. Economic indicators, many concerned simply with sheer volume such as the gross national product, or GNP, have been formulated to measure the progress of the economy. Production and profit have been the guiding principals of private enterprise, and "bigger and better" has become the slogan which best seems to capture the essence of the industrial spirit. Progress has come to be defined by size and novelty.

Initially many hoped that a high rate of technological growth could wipe out the massive poverty of the urban proletariat and reduce the social and economic inequalities in American society. While this proved to be an unrealistic expectation, America's increasing technological sophistication has managed to radically improve the standard of living for most citizens. People in high technology societies generally live more comfortably, eat better, and enjoy better medical care than people in the rest of the world.

University of Pennsylvania historian Charles Rosenberg's symposium on "Productivity as a Moral Absolute in America" examined this excessive preoccupation with production in American history as well as the possibility that the dysfunctional consequences of unrestrained technological innovation (like emotional alienation, environmental pollution and ecological imbalances) may mobilize people to seek political change. Members of his symposium discussed possible manifestations of such reaction in the increasing evidence of a renewed search for interpersonal intimacy and contact with nature and with the mysteries of the inner self among the young middle class. They also talked about the cultural possibilities and social psychological consequences of increased automation effecting a change in values from the work ethic to the cult of leisure and the capacity of developing nations to circumvent certain historical stages in their industrial growth and avoid some of the adverse consequences of "modernization."

The whole industrial-technological revolution has had profound consequences for the structure of American society. As mentioned, social and geographic mobility has led to the breakup of the extended family and the emergence of the modern nuclear family. The functions that the family performs for the larger society have been reduced to material consumption and primary socialization; and even the latter function has been taken over in large measure by the school, peer group and mass media. Similarly, the style of life in the family has been greatly altered by the introduction of mass produced, inexpensive household technology. Among other things, this has resulted in the obscuring of formerly clear life style distinctions between families of different social status.

The need to assimilate the millions of immigrants seeking work in industry and the increases in knowledge and skill required to work with and manage the new technology (plus the belief by the rich that education was an effective means of social control and by the poor that education was an effective means of increasing social equality) led to the institution of mass public education in the United States. More and more young people start school earlier and stay in school longer than ever before.

The curricula of the public schools have become increasingly diversified, while the overall structure has become increasingly uniform to meet the needs of an occupationally specialized, socially heterogeneous, geographically mobile work force. While the sterility and conformity in many American public schools have prompted critics to liken then to factories processing human commodities for the new technology, the new technology has made possible learning devices such as cheap paperbacks, audio-visual aids, and teaching machines which have allowed greater diversity in the modes and measures of learning.

The search for technological solutions to certain military and industrial problems has led to the invention and refinement of the electronic mass media. Television, perhaps the quintessential representative of the mass media, has become such an important part of American family life that many now consider it another instrument of child socialization. Considerable controversy has been generated over the content of the media and their potential effects on "impressionable minds." Some argue that the media are only capable of the most incidental of socialization since they can not directly reward learning and are often ancillary rather than central to other activities. At the least, however, proponents of this thesis are compelled to acknowledge the indirect effect TV has on the child's development by detracting from the time which would be spent in other activities (without making a judgment on the quality of these other activities).

Others argue that media like television have an ultimately beneficial effect on children since they can enlarge the viewer's frame of reference through the introduction of new ideas and role models. With respect to the violence controversy, TV's defenders argue that it has a cathartic effect on the viewer, allowing him to sublimate unconscious aggressions harmlessly through identification with TV heroes. Still others argue that TV has a malevolent effect on young

Americans because it presents a superficial and distorted view of American life (selectively ignoring important aspects of American society while pretending objectivity), distracts people from the true sources of their anxiety, and invites the emulation of violent behavior which is glorified by being presented as a legitimate and useful method of resolving conflict and achieving goals. Only research will ultimately provide the information required to arbitrate between these various points of view. The suggestion remains, however, that technology has in yet another way profoundly altered the experience of growing up in America.

The symposium on "Violence and the Mass Media," led by psychologist Klaus Scherer of the University of Pennsylvania, dealt with the above issue in addition to the role of the many relevant variables, such as the influence of primary groups, on the internalization of mass media norms and the relationship between the personality characteristics, social background, and intelligence of the viewer and his exposure and receptivity to the media. Also discussed were the phenomena of selective exposure, perception, and retention; the influence of pre-arousal on response to media violence; the capacity of children to distinguish reality from fantasy and the relative effectiveness of violence presented in these different contexts; and the relative effectiveness of rewarded, punished, inconsistently rewarded and/or ignored aggressive models on TV.

While the school, peer group, and mass media have emerged as important agents of socialization, the family and church have declined in their influence. Rapid cultural change due to technological innovation has reduced the relevance of the grandparent generation, and old people have been relegated to the obscurity of nursing homes. The father has been removed from the home for large periods of time, while the children spend more and more time in the company of peers and under the supervision of outside authorities. This leaves only the alternately bored and harried housewife as the strained nucleus of a weakened institution. The increasing pervasiveness of the rational, instrumental orientation which technology embodies has also undermined the mysticism and hierarchy of organized religion. Science has solved many of life's profoundest mysteries and is approaching solutions to the mystery of life itself. In an age of fertility drugs, artificial insemination, incubation in artifical wombs, cloning, chemical contraception, hygienic abortions, eugenics, and organ transplants, even the conventional notions of birth, life, and death must be redefined.

But just as technology has been used to produce life saving and labor saving devices, so has it been used to produce heinous poisons and instruments of mass destruction. Just as it has permitted man to harness and utilize the forces of nature to his own advantage, so has it halted the ultimately beneficial process of natural selection, polluted man's environment, and even threatened to destroy man's basic humanity.

The symposium on "The Genetic Manipulation of Future Generations," led by biologists Neville Kallenbach of the University of Pennsylvania and Barbara

Brownstein of Temple University, discussed some of these major positive and negative consequences of technology. Many in this symposium were concerned about the possible consequences of unrestrained military and industrial technology (such as increased radioactivity in the air and water, the increased resistance of bacteria to pharmaceutical control, and the problem of a demographic imbalance if parents are given the means to choose the sex of their child). Members of this symposium also examined the thorny political problems of pollution control, eugenics, and other issues; the socially inequitable distribution of the benefits of modern technology, particularly in the area of medical care; and the need for a government agency which has the competence that Congress lacks to supervise the rate and direction of technological growth and to plan for its consequences.

While it is very important to recognize that men in positions of authority in powerful institutions make decisions about what kinds of technology are to be developed for what purposes, it is also important to recognize that the technology that has been developed and the mere existence of an active technological capacity have deeply conditioned the nature of our existence. Machines have interdicted themselves between man and nature, between men and men, and even between man and himself. Technology has affected our language, habits, and modes of thought. As we have succeeded in reproducing some human processes in machine form so have we begun to think about and deal with human beings as machines. We put ourselves in "high gear" to perform the tasks that technology sets for us and "turn on," "tune in," and "drop out" when such tasks become boring and "turn us off." Paradoxically, those most concerned with improving the quality of their own interpersonal relationships, like sensitivity training group participants, talk about "static," "feedback," and "processing data." We shrink from needed institutional changes while allowing technology produced for private profit, but with obvious public consequences, to run rampant. Machines are invented to solve problems created by other machines. Technology, in effect, is allowed to set its own tasks irrespective of human values and human needs. Production has become a value in and of itself—a value which only makes sense in a society of private gain and public loss.

Philadelphia writer Ira Einhorn's symposium explored the relationship between "Technology and Consciousness," including the difference between linear and non-linear conceptions of reality. Einhorn stressed the need to make the current conditioning environment visible and to bring it under conscious individual control by using new metaphors and methods of perception while decentralizing the instruments of mass communication.

Some have pointed out that the effects of industrialization on American cultural patterns have been exaggerated and such things as the democratic family and romantic love complex, usually attributed to the effects of industrialization, have been shown to exist prior to the advent of industrialization. Nevertheless, the scope and pace of technological and social change in America today is unparalleled in history. It is no wonder that this loss of human community, absolute values, and firmly rooted personal identity has produced prophets and mystics who invite us to seek physical, spiritual, and emotional salvation through everything from drugs, transcendental meditation, spiritualism, and macrobiotics to Protestant fundamentalism. Art Rosenblum, of the Aquarian Research Foundation, told his symposium on "Psychic Research, Social Change, and the New Age" about the foundation's program of thought control which can allegedly teach people to control and remember their dreams and to read minds. He also discussed the scientific bases for Astrology and claimed that the Russians currently use it for birth control, assuring healthy babies, and choosing the sex of their children. He also discussed the possibility of life on the moon, life after death and contact with spirits, and heralded the rise of a new Era, forecast in the Bible, in which there would be peace, communal living, a sexual revolution, and women's liberation.

This historical scenario that we have drawn in the process of discussing the conference seminars points to certain crucial contemporary questions which were also discussed in the seminars. For one, there is the question of whether our current social and economic models, based on the notion of scarcity, are appropriate to governing human affairs in a society of abundance. Some argue that we have the technological capacity to significantly reduce human labor while adequately satisfying all the basic human needs of our citizenry. They say that the work ethic was and is yielding to a new cult of leisure in which men will be, more or less, liberated to pursue their own ends without fear of want. In significantly reducing or eliminating work, the argument goes, men will have to develop a new system for distributing resources (such as a guaranteed voucher system) and all forms of racial and political discrimination will be harder to maintain.

Others point out that a shortened work day has only made it possible for a substantial segment of the work force to get an extra job, that men have not been sufficiently educated to use their leisure in any creative fashion and that the primary source of identity for most people in America is still their occupational role. Still others argue that this technologically produced abundance is only superficial; that while constituting only 6 percent of the world's population, the United States consumes more than 50 percent of the world's resources; and that, despite this, there are still millions of hungry and sick Americans. Further speculation is raised as to how long the rest of the world will permit the United States and the other high technology societies to exploit their natural resources.

In questioning the feasibility of a plan, such as the guaranteed voucher system, others point out the difficulty of accurately defining or measuring an appropriate level of human need—especially in a stratified, achievement-oriented society in which advertising and recreation are major industries and status is symbolized by the conspicuous consumption of material goods. Still others continue to champion the alleged virtues of the Protestant ethic, oftentimes dressed up in the language of motivational psychology, and question whether one's standard of living shouldn't remain a privilege to be earned rather than a right to be guaranteed by the government.

Another issue has to do with the effect of modern technology on the structure of political decision making. Some argue that increasing industrial interdependence and national consciousness has required some centralization of decision making. They claim that a mass society can only be governed through representatives. They say that corporate price regulation, health and welfare, pollution control, and a great many other problems have shown themselves to be national in scope and, therefore, require federal supervision and control. While their opponents argue that new means of disseminating information to great numbers of people simultaneously has made it possible to begin to democratize decision making, they claim that only people with special expertise know how to utilize or manipulate such information effectively. Their opponents counter that this only allows technocrats to practice special interest politics under the guise of administration; that much of the information is not so highly technical; that expertise is also available in the community at large; and that, in any event, the public can be better educated to properly participate in such decision making. With cable television already here and two-way television close at hand, they assert, the means for providing direct democracy in a mass society are available. Still others argue that the means of mass dissemination of information should be used to enable individuals and small communities to utilize the benefits of improved data gathering and processing techniques to solve problems at the local level. According to them, the goal of our society should be to dismantle the giant, centralized bureaucracies and restore some efficacy to the individual and the small community.

This need to decentralize power by creating networks for coordinating information and resources, merging the university with its social environment, and increasing the level of public education was discussed by socioeconomist Robert Theobald in his symposium on "The Transition to the Cybernetic Era." Theobald maintained that, while a representative rather than direct democracy is necessary in a mass society, political officials are responsive to the electorate and are permitted to lead only so long as they meet the needs of the people. He talked about the struggle within all societies between synergetic (where people's desires and needs are congruent) and antropic (where people's desires and needs are contrary) forces and the need to improve our conscious decision-making capacity to the point where we can evaluate these forces accurately and not miss the decisions which need to be made. One key to the problem is contained in the awareness of different communication styles and the relative contribution of each to creating new insight as well as establishing a criteria and mode for efficient decision making.

Closely related to the issue of the distribution of power is the extent to which the public begins assuming responsibility for the rate and direction of technological development. Many still claim that profit motivated private enterprise is the soundest way to ensure plenty of high quality new goods. Others point out the monopolistic tendencies of capitalism and the extreme consequences of not holding private industry responsible for damage caused to the public sector. Still others also express concern for the fact that organizational efficiency takes precedence over worker satisfaction in private industry and, thus, many must sacrifice to benefit a few. These people feel that the public's political consciousness will be awakened by the dysfunctions of a technology not directly concerned with the public good. In any event, many people are feeling the need for government to develop and use some set of social indicators which attempt to measure the quality of life in addition to the current economic indicators, which simply measure the quantity of production.

Still another issue has to do with the feasibility and advisability of new social arrangements to reduce the institutional strains caused by rapid technological change. The high rate of divorce, emergence of the Women's Liberation Movement, and intensity of generational conflict would seem to suggest that the modern nuclear family may be one which makes excessive emotional claims on its members, frustrates the aspirations and potential of many women, and makes extreme demands on growing children, particularly adolescents. Universities are experiencing the acute tension between their imperatives to both transmit old knowledge and to create new knowledge, between honoring rationalism as well as tradition, between rewarding critical intellectual achievement while retaining the support of men in positions of power.

Finally, we must note a curious ambivalence in most of the discussants regarding technology—one which manifested itself in the way the participants would shift back and forth from gleefully cataloguing its astonishing achievements and bemoaning its terrible destructiveness. While this may reflect an ambivalence toward machines, dependency and social change which is deeply rooted in American cultural history, it also reflects the basic nature of technology itself.

There is no design or purpose in technology other than that given by men. What is also certain is that the scale of technological innovation and the scope of its effects are increasing rapidly in the Western world. We have created marvels and monsters of a size and dimension heretofore undreamed of; it is becoming increasingly imperative that we begin to assume responsibility and control of our machines and our destinies.

7

Summary of the Conference

In this final chapter we will not try to recapitulate the individual symposia or even the conference as a whole. What we will do is discuss certain themes which established their importance by being mentioned repeatedly by different speakers throughout the conference, overriding the formal distinctions of topics which officially defined the separate symposia.

In some of these cases there emerged an essential consensus regarding aspects of the relationship between technology and social change, while in others there was more obvious disagreement. In a very important way it is the disagreements which stand as the crucial contribution of the conference; they represent the important unanswered questions which point the way for future research. In matters of this sort, "agreement" and "disagreement" are better seen as relative positions on a continuum rather than as a dichotomy. In reviewing the themes which emerged in the conference we will move in the general direction from relatively greater agreement to relatively greater disagreement although, at certain points, logic and clarity will require detours from that path.

Technology and Social Change in History

It is surprising how often one encounters people who equate "technology" with "modern complex industrial technology" and then locate the origin of the relationship between technology and social change about 200 years ago. Several of the speakers helped this conference avoid committing that error. Melvin Kranzberg pointed out that many anthropologists define the human species on the basis of its tool dependency and that the beginnings of what we usually call "civilization" were dependent on the development of agricultural technology which dates back at least 10,000 years.

While Lewis Mumford denied that man's tool-making capacity was his most central characteristic, he also rejected the attempt to explain the relationship between technology and social change only on the basis of the events of the past 200 years. He viewed technology as an extension of the human organism and as being meaningless without man's subjective contributions. The relationship between man and technology, then, goes back to the beginnings of man. Even to find the source of the most current attitudes toward technology, one must, according to Mumford, go back 5,000 years to the Pyramid age. Important milestones in the relationship between man and technology can be found through all of the span of time between then and now. In a significant way, even the new wave of technological innovation can be dated back to the eleventh century. Even the crucial invention of mechanical timekeeping devices goes back to the fourteenth century.

There was some disagreement among speakers on the impact of technology on the quality of life. According to Victor Ferkiss, bureaucracy and administrative centralization, which were dependent on technological advances in communication and transportation, came into the world as liberating forces, more just and fair than the arbitrary rule of the local lords. Both Murray Bookchin and Kranzberg mentioned that because of material scarcity due to the limited development of technology throughout most of human history, most people have been forced to live at a bare subsistence level with no hope of anything better. Kranzberg further said that only very recently, as a result of technological development, has there been even the possibility of extending not only material comfort but also high culture to more than a very few. While Ashley Montagu did not dispute the long duration of the relationship between man and technology, he did argue that even the development of early agricultural technology upset the organic, biologically evolved relationships between man and man and man and nature. He said that in some sense the species has been in a precarious state ever since then.

Taken together, the separate elements of these views of the history of man and technology provide orientation for understanding the present day relationship between technology, the rest of culture, and man himself.

Technological Determinism and Human Nature

No speaker accepted any simple form of technological determinism; several explicitly rejected it. The most fully developed of these rejections was Seymour Melman's. He pointed out that machines do not design or build themselves and, even more importantly, there is no such thing as an inherently determined design for any class of machine. Design decisions must be made on what are ultimately non-technological grounds. Most often these criteria are economic, but they are also social and political. Melman emphasized the importance of understanding the social and political process by which technological decisions are made. By way of illustration he stressed the powerful role of the military in influencing the kind and level of technological research and development in the United States today. With slight differences of emphasis and detail, Robert Boguslaw, Melvin Kranzberg, and Nat Hentoff each made the same point: the key relationship is between man and man, not man and machine. Great confusion results from not properly distinguishing one type of relationship from the other.

Several speakers referred at different times to the work of Jacques Ellul, a French sociologist best known in the United States as the author of *The*

Technological Society. He is popularly identified as a technological determinist of a rather gloomy sort. Unfortunately the English title of his book does not describe its content or the real nature of his argument as well as does the original French title, *La Technique*. Ellul is talking not just about technology but about technique, which is a much broader, more encompassing phenomenon. Technique means any use of rationalized, standardized means in order to achieve a predetermined end. The principal elements of Lewis Mumford's megamachine, written records, mathematical notation, the concept of universal order, are excellent examples of technique which are not, by usual definition, technology. The pyramids of Egypt were built with the crudest of tools and machines, but by a society which was making great discoveries in social organization, mathematics, religion, and philosophy.

Ellul's concern is that the greater power of "technique" to achieve short term results will, in the long run, increasingly reshape and distort all of human culture into the mold of the most efficient and the most rational at the expense of other human qualities.

Ellul's argument about what he sees as the threat of technique does not appear to us to rest on ideas about the nature of technology or even ultimately on the nature of technique, although the latter is certainly of great importance. The argument rests, rather, on assumptions about the nature of man. To Ellul there is something about the character of man which makes him perceive the power of technique and to respond to it in the way he does. Mumford himself posed the questions: why has the power of the megamachine become greatest in Western culture and, even more important, why have we in the modern West developed the idea that we must conform to the dictates of technology (and of other aspects of technique) and establish our priorities strictly on the basis of technological potential, as in the space program for example. However he rejected the idea that man has any innate drive toward technological innovation. He cited examples of many human cultures which have suffered because they were too resistant to experimentation. A line of explanation for the apparently irresistible nature of technological possibilities other than an innate drive toward innovation is the role of special interest groups. For example, Melvin Kranzberg pointed to the role of certain groups in search of profit in explaining the support for the development of the supersonic transport plane (the SST). While some research has been done on playful experimentation by children and non-human primates, there is none which we know of focused directly on the question of an innate drive toward technological innovation in adult humans. This remains an area for further research at the psycho-physiological level.

In rejecting the simple forms of technological determinism, several speakers made use of the concept of cultural values. Robert Boguslaw said that humanistic values could not be threatened by technology, but only by other, anti-humanistic values. E. Digby Baltzell pointed to the different American and British values toward tradition and authority in discussing their different attitudes toward the use of technology. Melvin Tumin discussed the importance of the values of progress and democracy in American history and the present impact of the values of existentialism, moral and cultural relativism, Marxism, psychoanalysis, and progressive education on American culture. In all these examples, and we could cite even more, the basic point is the same. Man's use of technology is ultimately determined by his values—not just his values about technology, but his values about almost everything. Tumin made this point most explicitly with his diagram which suggested the interrelationship not only between technology and values, but also with human and natural resources, social organization, and cultural themes as well.

While introducing the concept of value helps avoid the error Seymour Melman warned against of failing to distinguish between man-man and man-machine relationships, it still only allows us to begin to trace out the complex interrelationships between particular values and the utilization of particular forms of technology. Just consider, for example, the maze of values, briefly touched on by Melman and by Melvin Kranzberg, which surrounds the manufacture and use of automobiles in the United States. Another example of the relationship between values, political interests, and technology which Melman cited is the contrast between the post-World War II development of technology in the United States and Japan. While the United States has concentrated on military technology, it was left to Japan to develop high quality, low cost consumer goods, especially in areas such as electronics.

A number of speakers mentioned a possible connection between technology or technological values and the values of the current counterculture. Murray Bookchin pointed to the large number of people seeking small scale communities and alternative lifestyles as evidence of an increasing rejection of the values of industrial era technology. Max Lerner stated his agreement with many of these so-called countercultural values and credited the counterculture with helping to resist the internalization of technological values to a dangerous degree in the culture as a whole.

Seymour Martin Lipset vigorously denied that the current counterculture is a response to contemporary technology. Invoking what he called the "law of limited possibilities," he pointed to a long list of previous countercultures going back as far as the early nineteenth century, which shared many of the life style characteristics of the present one. Moreover, he pointed out that for well over fifty years analysts have been suggesting that the response to technology or technological change has been the cause of countercultures. Taking issue with Lipset, Nat Hentoff argued that, within his broader definition of the counter-culture, there is evidence of real institutional change. Hentoff, however, did not clearly tie his analysis of the counterculture to the question of technology.

Lipset, Hentoff, and Edgar Friedenberg all discussed the counterculture in relation to the prospect for political change, particularly revolutionary political change. Friedenberg, whose definition of the counterculture was initially limited to what he called the "hippie communal life style," conceded that its values were essentially elitist. He granted that the impact of this elitism is probably counter-revolutionary in a narrowly political sense, but maintained that revolutions usually do not affect very basic changes and that what is needed is a more profound, evolutionary form of social change. Robert Theobald made the same judgment on the distinction between revolution and evolution. Max Lerner said that he thinks the United States is today a very revolutionary society, but his remarks made it clear that what he meant was that the United States is in a state of flux and is receptive to at least some of the kinds of evolutionary changes that Theobald and Friedenberg spoke about. Murray Bookchin expressed the concern that the changes taking place now in American society are not all progressive, but some are highly reactionary, and that we must be very aware of this as well.

The question of the relationship between man and technology was repeatedly recast into the question of the nature of man. As mentioned, a large part of Lewis Mumford's keynote address concerned the nature of man. Max Lerner also began by saying that to him the nature of man and the nature of society were the two crucial questions. He pointed out that the nature of man has always had its dark side, that it does no good to try to ascribe all the bad in the world to modern technology, or bureaucracy, or any of several other currently popular villains. He expressed a concern about the internalization of technological values, or more accurately, the values of technique, but again emphasized that the key point is that the internalization of these or any values is dependent on the character of man. Lerner did say that changes in technology often set off other social changes, but his emphasis on the nature of man and the actual process of social change prevents his position from being one of simple technological determinism.

Melvin Kranzberg also discussed the relationship between technology and the nature of man. In his opening literary references, he showed that in both the case of Frankenstein's monster and the case of the Universal robots, the ultimate tragedies resulted from human flaws, not technological ones. The Janus-faced nature of technology, its apparent potential for both good and evil, actually no more than represents the nature of man himself. The significance of technology lies in its use by humans. Warfare has been part of human history from the beginning and it has never been the case that rifles have fired themselves. Therefore, if man is somehow doomed by technology, it is not because of the nature of technology, but because of the nature of man. And the question is not just one of good and evil. Kranzberg pointed out that all men's intentions appear justified to them, no matter how evil they might strike someone else. The concern, rather, is with more specific aspects of individual motivation and the ways men relate to other men.

An important example of the significance of the structure of human relationships in understanding social change lies in the balance between cooperation and competition. Mumford showed how the discovery of the megamachine allowed men to organize themselves in a hierarchical fashion, based on competition and unequal power, to do things they had been unable to do before. This competitive struggle for power also led to repeated cultural destruction. In a world with limited technology, the consequences of destruction were never too great; in a world with nuclear technology they might well be.

None of the speakers denied that competitive behavior has played a major role in human history. However several did question whether it is a fundamental part of human nature. Murray Bookchin argued most explicitly that, while competitive behavior may have been functional in a time of economic scarcity, it is not an intrinsic part of human nature and should be eliminated in an era of abundance. Without being as explicit, Ashley Montagu declared that man's purpose on earth was to live as if to live and to love were one.

While he did not link it specifically to the question of human nature, Seymour Melman did cite the results of his comparative research which showed that manufacturing enterprises on Israeli kibbutzim which used cooperative rather than hierarchical decision-making schemes actually had higher productivity than technologically equivalent factories in other places.

Melvin Kranzberg used automobile pollution as an example of a problem which is created by individuals separately pursuing their own ends in a way which only becomes dangerous once a threshold level is passed. This is an example of a case where it obviously is true that no one person's motives are evil nor acts destructive. The problem is not caused by any one individual driving his car; it is caused when the total number of cars being driven passes the pollution threshold level. There are many other similar examples where the use of modern technology becomes a social problem only once a threshold level is passed. This type of problem has both competitive and cooperative solutions, so our ability to survive them is not directly dependent on how competitive or cooperative man is by nature. However, in the years to come, problems like this increasingly may force public attention on the issue of competition or cooperation and serve to expose the locations and distribution of social power.

Technology and the Environment

The focus of the conference was very clearly on the United States and, by extension, other highly industrialized societies. A number of speakers, however, did place questions of population size, ecology, and abundance in a worldwide context. Robert Theobald, Melvin Tumin, and Seymour Martin Lipset all pointed out that the whole world population, even at its present size, is dependent on advanced technology and bureaucratic organization. This, in itself, rules out a return to simpler forms of technology. The challenge, instead, is to find ways of limiting further growth in a population which is still increasing very rapidly in size. Several speakers mentioned Kenneth Boulding's distinction between the open, cowboy economy of the past and the closed, spaceman or spaceship economy we must plan for in the future.

No speaker disagreed with the idea that we must now be concerned with questions of ecology and environmental quality. Lipset and Kranzberg however both pointed to the political and ethical problems of rich nations, such as the United States, insisting on a clean environment which, however necessary it may be to the entire planet in the long run, would cost poor countries much more than rich ones in the short run. In the United States the use of DDT is not a question of life or death for human beings this year, while in India it is. Theobald and Victor Ferkiss also both expressed concern about this world conflict between the rich and poor nations which is also a conflict between white and non-white peoples. One of the paradoxes of modern times is that, as the world has been made smaller by improvements in communications, the differences between peoples in terms of the material standard of living, health, and life expectancy itself have become vastly greater than ever before.

In speaking about the SST decision, Theobald warned that while some people were hailing it as a sign that finally ecological issues were going to receive their proper attention and that national priorities were changing, there was a real danger that we might just be replacing one absolutist mind set by another. It is important that we do get away from the idea that anything that science and technology can do is good and should be done, but it is just as important that we not develop the opposite attitude that science and technology are bad and that innovation should be discouraged.

Technology and Abundance

Much has been said and written in recent years about the social implications of material abundance. Most of the speakers at this conference did not address the question of abundance directly, but those who did took a variety of quite different positions about it. Several also anchored their arguments about such issues as bureaucracy, hierarchy, centralization, elitism, and authority to their positions on abundance.

Robert Theobald and Murray Bookchin stated that we have reached, or very shortly will reach, the potential for abundance for all citizens in the United States. Bookchin argued that, with abundance, there is no further need for a concern with efficiency as the highest value and, therefore, no need for the forms of social organization which limit the freedom and opportunities of individuals in the name of overall efficiency. According to him, we already have the technology required to live as well as we could wish in small scale decentralized communities. This pattern of life would not require hierarchical, bureaucratic organization. He further suggested that we are not now making use of this technology precisely because it would challenge the present distribution of political and economic power.

Theobald reminded us that the basic assumption of economics in the past has been scarcity. If you start instead with the assumption of abundance, the entire picture changes. For one thing, it no longer works to use job holding as the basis for allocating goods and services. Theobald also related abundance to broader changes in social organization by an analysis of a change in the basis of authority. For reasons which include the sheer rapidity of change itself and the tremendous increase in our capacity to organize and communicate information, the basis for authority is changing from structural position to possession of knowledge. In the future we can expect that increasingly people will be attended to on the basis of what they actually know rather than the bureaucratic or hierarchical position they hold. Charles Dechert also explored the potential impact of computers on social organization and possible changes in the nature of work and job holding, although he did not take the kind of explicit position on abundance that Bookchin and Theobald did.

Victor Ferkiss disputed Bookchin's assumption of abundance by pointing out that at the most technology is now over-producing for only a minority of Americans. Not only is the picture one of great scarcity on a worldwide basis, but even within the United States there is still tremendous poverty. Moreover, certain things, like ocean beach front, are inherently limited and will always be in short supply.

The arguments concerning abundance really revolve around three related questions. The first question is whether or not we presently enjoy or at least have the technological capacity to create abundance for all in the United States. Here the definition of abundance is crucial. If by abundance we mean the capacity to supply everyone's basic subsistence needs (and perhaps a little more), then many would agree we now have it. If, however, we mean the ability to supply everything that anyone could possibly desire without more than a handful of people having to work, then certainly not very many people would agree we now have such a technological capacity. The question of the economic relationship of the United States and other rich countries with the rest of the world also enters in at this level.

The second question concerning abundance is whether or not we will ever have it. Some who do not believe we have yet achieved abundance by any definition concede that we might at some future time. Others point to the great plasticity of human needs and desires and the difficulty of predicting the demand for things which have not even been invented yet. They argue that the ability to provide a subsistence living for everyone is not grounds enough to alter the entire foundation of economics. This question also includes points like Ferkiss's about the inherent scarcity of some things which are highly desired. The ability of advertising to create material wants (as well as the ethics of its doing so) also are relevant here.

The third question starts from the possibility of future abundance and asks will it, can it, or should it have the kinds of consequences that Theobald and

Bookchin suggest it will. A science fiction picture of abundance very different from either of theirs is one of a highly centralized, bureaucratic society providing an endless supply of goods and services to a people who, while exempt from toil, are also without real freedom. The third question allows the opportunity to think through the implications of abundance without necessarily having to take a position on the first two questions.

Although the question of abundance did not draw as much attention at the conference as did questions of the nature of man, it is also a crucial question concerning technology, power, and social change about which there was sharp disagreement among the speakers.

Technology and Social Organization

The interrelated questions of bureaucracy, hierarchy, and elitism were also discussed in other contexts. In each case the discussion focused on the same question which Theobald and Bookchin raised as part of their presentations: "Do changes in communications and information technology make traditional patterns of bureaucracy, hierarchy, and elite authority unnecessary and therefore obsolete?" As we have already seen, Theobald and Bookchin said yes. Dechert suggested that improved technology may allow the replacement of traditional hierarchical communication in large scale organizations by dense webs of communication.

In what was the most direct and spirited clash of opinion among the speakers at the conference, Max Lerner disagreed with Murray Bookchin and maintained that leadership and authority will always be necessary, regardless of the increasingly widespread availability of information for decision making. According to Lerner, if one social group abdicates its authority, another will take its place. Melvin Tumin said that even with instantaneous communication, specialists and experts will still be needed, but it is a different question as to whether or not they need constitute a political or class elite. E. Digby Baltzell, on the other hand, argued for the need for elite leadership and authority in society and drew attention to the relationship between leadership and authority and the establishment of norms and values for a society. He pointed out specific ways in which differences between American and British attitudes toward hierarchical authority might relate to differences in their attitudes toward technology.

The discussion of centralization was rather overshadowed by the discussions of hierarchy and elitism and did not attract the same degree of passion. Murray Bookchin strongly promoted the value of decentralization, maintaining that advanced technology is now making it possible again. Robert Theobald, Victor Ferkiss, and Charles Dechert were more cautious. Each pointed out ways in which some technological changes have centralizing effects while others have decentralizing effects.

The one point which all the speakers repeatedly expressed was that our concern should be with man—his nature, his needs, his relationship with other men and with the environment. There is no autonomous force in technology itself which has any control over us. If Ellul is right about the susceptibility of man to technique, to the power of the rational, that susceptibility lies somewhere in the nature of man, not in the nature of technique.

As several speakers said explicitly, there is no such thing as "the machine" in the abstract. Whenever we look at specific examples of technology, we are also looking at the acts of specific men who have certain goals and values and are interracting with other men who have their own goals and values. The questions of good and evil, competition and cooperation, hierarchy and equality are questions having to do with the relations of men to men and of the social power expressed in those relations. Technology is a part of culture. Man's cultural adaptation to the environment is a unique evolutionary experiment. Man's ability to manage the extensions of himself which technology represent will be an increasingly important measure of the success of this experiment.

About the Contributors

E. Digby Baltzell, born in 1915, is Professor of Sociology at the University of Pennsylvania. He received his Ph.D. in Sociology from Columbia University in 1952. His major historical works on stratification in America, *Philadelphia Gentleman* (1958) and *The Protestant Establishment* (1964) are considered classics in his field.

Robert Boguslaw, born in 1919, is Professor of Sociology at Washington University at St. Louis. He received his Ph.D. in Sociology from New York University. His publications include "The Design Perspective in Sociology," in W. Bell and J.A. Mau (eds.), *The Sociology of the Future* (New York: Russell Sage Foundation, 1971); "Social Action and Social Change," in Erwin O. Smigel (ed.) *Handbook on the Study of Social Problems* (Chicago: Rand McNally, 1971); and *The New Utopians: A Study of System Design and Social Change* (Englewood Cliffs, New Jersey: Prentice-Hall, 1965), for which he won the C. Wright Mills award from the Society for the Study of Social Problems.

Murray Bookchin is an anarchist who has been active in radical movements over the past forty years. He is the author of *Post-Scarcity Anarchism* (1971), *Crisis in Our Cities* (1965), and *Our Synthetic Environment* (1962).

Charles R. Dechert, born in 1927, is Ordinary Professor of Politics at the Catholic University of America. He received his Ph.D. in Social and Political Philosophy at The Catholic University of America in 1952. His books range from *Thomas More and Society* (1952) to *The Social Impact of Cybernetics* (1967), for which he is both editor and contributor.

Ira Einhorn, born in 1940, describes himself as a "planetary enzyme." He received his B.A. in English at the University of Pennsylvania and has authored "The Sociology of the Now," in Bernard Aaronson and Humphrey Osmand (eds.), *Psychedelics* (1970), as well as "Ecological Theatre: The Night of Neoplasm," in Edward Rice and Jane Garmey (eds.), *The Prophetic Generation.*

Victor C. Ferkiss, born in 1925, is Professor of Government at Georgetown University. He received his Ph.D. in Sociology from the University of Chicago. He is the author of *African Search for Identity* (1966) and *Technological Man: The Myth and the Reality* (1969).

Edgar Z. Friedenberg, born in 1921, is Professor of Education at Dalhousie University. He received his Ph.D. in Education from the University of Chicago in 1946. He is the author of *The Vanishing Adolescent* (1959), *Coming of Age in*

America (1963), *The Anti-American Generation* (1971) of which he is editor, and numerous articles and reviews on education in America which have appeared in *The New York Review of Books* and other leading publications.

Nat Hentoff, born in 1925, is a writer for the *Village Voice, Downbeat, Playboy, Evergreen Review*, and other national magazines. He received his B.A. from Northeastern University in 1945 and went on to do post-graduate work at Harvard. He is a recognized expert on jazz music and a respected observer of the youth and black scene. His books include *The Jazz Makers* (1957), *The Peace Agitator* (1963), and *Black Anti-Semitism and Jewish Racism* (1970), of which he is both editor and contributor.

Melvin Kranzberg, born in 1917, is Director of the Graduate Program in History of Science and Technology at Case Western Reserve University. He received his Ph.D. in History from Harvard University. He is Editor-in-Chief of *Technology and Culture*, a quarterly journal of The Society for the History of Technology, and has authored the two volume work, *Technology in Western Civilization* (1967).

Max Lerner, born in 1902, is Professor of American Civilization at Brandeis University. He is also a nationally syndicated columnist, author, and lecturer. He received his Ph.D. from the Robert Brookings Graduate School of Economics and Government in 1927. His many books include *America as a Civilization* (1957), *The Unfinished Country* (1959), and *The Age of Overkill* (1962).

Seymour Martin Lipset, born in 1922, is Professor of Government and Sociology at Harvard University. He received his Ph.D. in Sociology from Columbia University in 1949. He has written several books on politics, economics, and social change. His most recent publications are *Rebellion in the University* (1972) and the *Politics of Unreason* (1970). The latter, co-authored with Earl Raab, received the Gunnar Myrdal Prize for 1970.

Seymour Melman, born in 1917, is Professor of Industrial Engineering at Columbia University, where he received his Ph.D. in Economics. His many works include *Decision-Making and Productivity* (1958), *The Peace Race* (1961), *Our Depleted Society* (1965), and *Pentagon Capitalism* (1970).

Ashley Montagu, born in 1905, is an internationally known author and lecturer. He was formerly Chairman of the Department of Anthropology at Rutgers University. He received his Ph.D. in Anthropology from Columbia University in 1937. His many books include *On Being Human* (1950), *The Natural Superiority of Women* (1953), *Man in Process* (1961), and *The Idea of Race* (1965).

Lewis Mumford, born in 1895, is an internationally known author and lecturer on technology and history. He holds an Honorary LL.D. from the University of Edinburgh and an Honorary Ph.D. in Architecture from the University of Rome. His writings have been widely read for over forty years. His most recent publications include *The City in History* (1961), *Technics and Human Development* (1967), and *The Pentagon of Power* (1971).

Jerold M. Starr, born in 1941, is Assistant Professor of Sociology at the University of Pennsylvania. He received his Ph.D. in Sociology from Brandeis University in 1970, where his dissertation was entitled *Cross-Cultural Encounter and Personality Change: Peace Corps Volunteers in the Philippines.* He is author of "Some Sociological Issues in International Development," presented at the VII World Congress of Sociology at Varna, Bulgaria (1970) and is currently editing a text and reader on *Character and Social Structure*, to be published by Little, Brown and Company in 1973.

Robert Theobald, born in 1929, is an author, consultant, and often quoted authority on economics and technology. He received an M.A. in Economics from Cambridge University. His most recent works include *Habit and Habitat* (1972), *Teg's 1994* (1971), which he co-authored with J.M. Scott, and *Futures Conditional* (1972), of which he is editor.

Charles A. Thrall, born in 1942, is Assistant Professor of Sociology at the University of Pennsylvania. He received his Ph.D. in Sociology from Harvard University in 1970, where his dissertation was titled *Household Technology and the Division of Labor in Families.* His papers include "Attitudes of the American Protestant Clergy Towards Issues of War and Peace," *Fellowship* (1964) and "Impairment of Psychiatric Outpatients and Change with Treatment," *Mental Hygiene* (1964). He is now studying the relationship between technological change, urbanization, and the role of casual labor in the job structure.

Melvin M. Tumin, born in 1919, is Professor of Sociology and Anthropology at Princeton University. He received his Ph.D. in Sociology and Anthropology from Northwestern University in 1944. His numerous publications include *Social Life: Structure and Function* (1948), *Desegregation: Resistance and Readiness* (1958), *Social Stratification* (1967), and *Crimes of Violence: Causes and Preventions* (1969).

DATE DUE

F			
MY 4 '77			
NO 28 77			
DE 13 '77			
DE 20 '77			
AP 25 '78			
AP 25 '78			
			.
GAYLORD			PRINTED IN U.S.A.